AN
ENGLISH GRAMMAR

AN ENGLISH GRAMMAR

GEORGE CURREY

GYAN

Published by

Gyan Publishing House
5, Ansari Road
Daryaganj, New Delhi-110002
Phone: 011-47034999, 9811692060
E-mail: books@gyanbooks.com

Distribution Network
gyanbooks.com
India, USA, Canada, UK, Australia

ISBN: 978-93-6920-282-9 (PB)

First Published, 1856

2nd Impression 2025

Printed at: Gyan Press, Delhi.

AN ENGLISH GRAMMAR
Author: GEORGE CURREY

AN ENGLISH GRAMMAR,

FOR THE USE OF SCHOOLS.

BY THE REV. GEORGE CURREY,

PREACHER AT THE CHARTERHOUSE, LONDON.

PUBLISHED UNDER THE DIRECTION OF
THE COMMITTEE OF GENERAL LITERATURE AND EDUCATION,
APPOINTED BY THE SOCIETY FOR PROMOTING
CHRISTIAN KNOWLEDGE.

LONDON:
Printed for the
SOCIETY FOR PROMOTING CHRISTIAN KNOWLEDGE;
SOLD AT THE DEPOSITORIES,
GREAT QUEEN STREET, LINCOLN'S INN FIELDS,
4, ROYAL EXCHANGE, AND 16, HANOVER STREET, HANOVER SQUARE;
AND AT THE
NATIONAL SOCIETY'S DEPOSITORY, WESTMINSTER;
AND BY ALL BOOKSELLERS.
1856.

PREFACE.

THIS work does not attempt to discuss the *principles* of Grammar further than is necessary in order to give *definite rules*. It is hoped that most of the ordinary constructions in the English language have been noticed.

A "Grammar for Schools" must of necessity be adapted for pupils of various ages and attainments; and the teacher must use his discretion as to the parts to which the attention of each class is to be directed. In order to facilitate his selection, the principal rules are numbered, and printed with a difference of type. They are collected together in Chap. XVII., so as to be more readily learnt by heart.

An intelligent teacher will be aware that no Grammar can dispense with the neccssity of oral instruction. Each rule must be illustrated by examples, which may be taken from the Reading Books used in the school. It is recommended that as soon as possible the children be exercised in parsing easy sentences—the easier the better to begin with. To more advanced pupils Poetry will be found especially useful in teaching them to supply ellipses, and to recognize the several parts of a sentence when they occur in an inverted order.

The simple direction in "The Schoolmaster" of Roger Ascham cannot be too carefully attended to. "Let him (the schoolmaster) construe it into English so often as the children may easily carry away the understanding of it; lastly, parse it over perfectly. This done thus, by and by, let the child construe and parse it over again." Ascham is indeed speaking of Latin, but the same method may be very profitably employed in English, if instead of *construing*, a clear explanation be given of each sentence, word by word. It is by a knowledge of Grammar that we are able to examine a sentence, and so to understand it more perfectly than we could otherwise do; and continual exercise in *parsing* is the point upon which instruction in Grammar chiefly turns.

The simpler portions of this Grammar have been collected and published in a separate form, under the title of "A Grammar for Beginners;" which will be most useful in the lower classes, and will form the best introduction to the study of the present "Grammar for Schools."

Examples of *parsing* are given in each Grammar.

CONTENTS.

PART II. SYNTAX.

APPENDIX I.

APPENDIX II.

EXPLANATIONS OF SIGNS USED IN THIS BOOK.

N.B. stands for *nota bene*, which means, *take notice.*

i. e. stands for *id est*, which means, *that is.*

viz. stands for *videlicet*, which means, *that is to say.*

e. g. stands for *exempli gratiâ*, which means, *by way of example, for instance.*

obs. stands for *obsolete*, which means, *disused, gone out of use.*

&c. stands for *et cætera*, which means, *and the rest.*

" " These marks are called inverted commas. They show that the words between them are borrowed from some other book, or part of this book, or are to be noticed particularly.

( ) These marks are called *brackets.* They show that what is enclosed between them is taken out of the sentence and set by itself. The words between them are called a *parenthesis.*

§ This mark stands at the head of every fresh *section* or portion into which the chapters are divided.

INTRODUCTION

THE SOURCES OF THE ENGLISH LANGUAGE.

THE present English language proceeds, in the main, from the language spoken by the Anglo-Saxon nation; that is, the nation which was composed of those tribes who began to occupy Britain about the year 449 after Christ.

These tribes are known by the names of Jutes, Angles, and Saxons. They all came from countries nearly adjoining each other in the north of Germany and Denmark, and spoke languages which had a strong common resemblance; but as the Jutes were the least powerful, the speech of the conquerors of Britain came to be called English-Saxon or Anglo-Saxon.

The inhabitants whom the Anglo-Saxons had subdued were of the Celtic race. Their languages were divided into Celtic or Gaelic, and British or Cambrian. Gaelic in some form or other is still spoken in the Highlands of Scotland; in Ireland; and in the Isle of Man, where, it is called Manx. The British language is spoken by the Welsh people, who call themselves Cymry. A language closely resembling this is found in the province of Brittany in France.

The Romans, who had possessed the greater part of Britain for about 300 years before the coming of the Saxons, made very little change in the ancient languages; but the Latin language has since that time entered largely into the substance of English.

This has come to pass, partly in consequence of the Norman Conquest, A.D. 1066, and partly from other causes.

The Normans, who were of the same

race as the Danes or Northmen, who so often invaded England, spoke originally a language not unlike that of the Anglo-Saxons; but they lost their own language when they conquered Normandy, and learned to speak French.

For more than 200 years after the Conquest the majority of the people of England spoke Anglo-Saxon; but French was employed in most public transactions until the 14th century. During this time also, as had been the case long before the Conquest, Latin, from which French is mainly derived, was the language of the Church and clergy; and it has been for many purposes employed by a large number of people up to the present time. The Latin language therefore, both directly and indirectly, has acquired an extensive influence over the English.

But in the mean time, and from causes independent of the Norman Conquest, the Saxon language of our ancestors underwent changes, by which it has become by degrees that which is now called English; but with a large mixture of words proceeding from French, Latin, and other languages, to which others also are being constantly added from various sources.

Changes of a like nature have taken place in other European languages which belong to the same general class as Anglo-Saxon and English.

It will be of use to us in studying English to remember these facts; as we shall thereby be enabled to account for various usages which might otherwise seem strange and unaccountable.

ENGLISH GRAMMAR.

PART I.

CHAPTER I.

§ 1. THE words which we use in expressing our thoughts, and the manner in which those words are put together, make up what is called LANGUAGE.

GRAMMAR is that branch of knowledge which teaches us to write or speak any language correctly.

Grammar consists of two parts—

1. ACCIDENCE, the part which teaches us the formation and classification of words.

2. SYNTAX, the part which teaches us how to put words together.

LETTERS—SYLLABLES—WORDS.

§ 2. The different sounds of the voice are expressed in writing by LETTERS.

There are twenty-six Letters in English, which taken together we call the Alphabet—

a, b, c, d, e, f, g, h, i, j, k, l, m, n, o, p, q, r, s, t, u, v, w, x, y, z.

This way of printing is called ROMAN.

Sometimes they are printed thus—

a, b, c, x, y, z.

This way of printing is called ITALIC.

The large letters, which are called CAPITAL letters, are printed thus—

A, B, C (Roman).
A, B, C (Italic).

Five letters are called VOWELS or voice-letters, because they alone can be sounded by themselves—

a, e, i, o, u.

Twenty-one are CONSONANTS, because in order to be *sounded* they must have a vowel *with* them—

b, c, d, f, g, h, j, k, l, m, n, p, q, r, s, t, v,
w, x, y, z.

Of these twenty-one, two, *w*, *y*, are called SEMI-VOWELS, that is, *half-vowels*.

One, *h*, is called the ASPIRATE or *rough-breathing*; which is sounded at the beginning in most words. In the following it is not sounded, and is then said to be silent—

heir,
honour, honest,
humour,
hour.

E is generally silent at the end of a word, as *give*, *life*; sometimes likewise in the middle of a word, as *ungrateful*. It often lengthens the preceding vowel, as *bĭd, bīde;* sometimes it softens a preceding *c* or *g*, as *justice, judge, vestige.*

Two vowels, or a vowel and a semi-vowel joined together in one syllable, have the name of DIPHTHONG—

æ, œ, which are found only in words derived from Greek or Latin.

ai, ay, au, aw,
ea, ee, ei, ey, eu, ew,
ie,
oa, oi, oy, oo, ou, ow,
ua, ui, ue,
} are Diphthongs.

Three vowels joined together make what is called a TRIPHTHONG—

ieu, iew, eau, are Triphthongs.

Vowels by themselves, or vowels with consonants, make SYLLABLES.

WORDS consist of one or more than one syllable.

Words of one syllable are called MONOSYLLABLES; words of two syllables are called DISSYLLABLES; words of more syllables than two are called POLYSYLLABLES.

The stress which we lay on particular syllables in speaking is called ACCENT.

Accent is very seldom marked in printing or in writing, unless we wish to notice it particularly.

CHAPTER II.

PARTS OF SPEECH.

§ 3. THERE are nine sorts of words, or as they are commonly called PARTS OF SPEECH.

1. Nouns Substantive, or SUBSTANTIVES. These are names of persons, places, or things, Noun means *name*. *John*, *meat*, *man*, *tree*, are substantives.

2. Nouns Adjective, or ADJECTIVES; words added to substantives, and are the names of qualities belonging to them; as *dear*, *green*, *honest*.

3. PRONOUNS; words used instead of nouns, as *I*, *you*, *it*.

4. ARTICLES; the words *an*, *a*, *the*.

5. VERBS, or chief words in speech.

Verbs either express *being*, as *am*, *be;* or express *doing*, as *walk*, *eat*, *run*.

The remaining parts of speech are called Particles.

6. PREPOSITIONS; particles set before substantives, or words used as substantives, to show their relation to other words, as *to*, *by*, *with*.

7. CONJUNCTIONS; particles used to join sentences together, as *and*, *as*, *but*, *although*, &c.

8. ADVERBS; particles added to verbs, adjectives, or other adverbs, to express some circumstance belonging to them, as *very*, *slightly*.

9. INTERJECTIONS; exclamations, as *oh! alas! hollo!*

The nine parts of speech then are:— 1. Noun Substantive. 2. Noun Adjective. 3. Pronoun. 4. Article. 5. Verb. 6. Adverb. 7. Preposition. 8. Conjunction. 9. Interjection.

CHAPTER III.

SUBSTANTIVES.—NUMBER.

§ 4. NOUNS Substantive, or SUBSTANTIVES, are names of persons, places, or things, of which we can think by themselves.

The names of particular persons or places are called PROPER NAMES:—

John, London, Herefordshire.

The names which belong to classes of persons or of things are called COMMON NOUNS:—

spade, bull, friend, river.

The names of *qualities* are called ABSTRACT NOUNS:—

virtue, happiness.

Nouns which point out a number of persons or things collected into one body are called COLLECTIVE NOUNS, as *army, corporation.*

Substantives are often made up or compounded of two substantives—

schoolroom, railway, candlestick.

In some compound substantives it is usual to place a - (called *hyphen*) between the two parts of the word—

tea-chest, hearth-brush, arm-chair.

NUMBER.

§ 5. When one thing or person is spoken of at a time, the noun is said to be in the SINGULAR NUMBER.

Thus: *boy*, i.e. one boy, is Singular.

When more than one are spoken of at a time, a letter or syllable is generally added to the word, and it is then said to be in the PLURAL NUMBER.

Thus: *boys*, i.e. more than one boy, is Plural.

Nouns substantive therefore have two numbers, the Singular and the Plural.

The plural number generally ends in *s*, as hill, *hills*; tree, *trees*; shape, *shapes*.

Compound substantives change only the last substantive, *arm-chairs, school children.*

Most words ending in a vowel make the

plural in *s*, except words in *o*, which generally add *es*, as echo, *echoes*; hero, *heroes*.

But some words in *o* only add *s*, as folio, *folios*; piano, *pianos*.

Words in *s*, *sh*, *ch*, *x*, make the plural in *es*; and this plural ending forms a separate syllable, as pass, *pass-es*; rush, *rush-es*; church, *church-es*; fox, *fox-es*.

In words in *ce*, *ge*, *se*, and *ze*, though they only add *s* for the plural, the ending *es* forms an additional syllable, as prince, *princes*; judge, *judges*; rose, *roses*; prize, *prizes*.

When a word ends in *y* with a vowel before it, *s* only is added, as *monkey*, *monkeys*; *money*, *moneys*; *journey*, *journeys*; *day*, *days*. But if a consonant come before *y* the *y* is changed into *ie*, as *fly*, *flies*; *city*, *cities*.

Some words change *f* and *fe* into *ves*, as *calf*, *calves*; *wife*, *wives*; *wolf*, *wolves*.

Penny makes *pence*, and also *pennies*.

Die makes *dice*, but when it means a stamp for coining it makes *dies*.

The following words form their plural thus:—

goose	*geese*	tooth	*teeth*
louse	*lice*	foot	*feet*
mouse	*mice*	cow	*cows* or *kine*
man	*men*	child	*children*
ox	*oxen*	brother	*brothers* or *brethren*

Proper names in general make no change of form in the plural number. If the same proper name belong to more than one person mentioned, we express it thus: *John and Susan Smith*, not *Smiths; Julius and Augustus Cæsar.*

If, however, only one proper name is used, and we wish to mention several individuals who bear that name, the final *s* is added: *the Edwards, the Cæsars, the Herods.*

Such a phrase as *the Misses Johnson* is more correct than *the Miss Johnsons,* although the latter may be admitted, because in that case we consider *Miss-Johnson* as a compound substantive, and speak of more than one *Miss-Johnson.*

§ 6. Many words have no change in the plural, as *sheep, deer, salmon, grouse.*

Some are commonly used in the plural without change, as *pair, ton, pound,* though it is more correct to say *pairs, tons, pounds.*

Some words are not used in the singular, as *tongs, snuffers, bellows, stilts.*

Some are scarcely ever used in the plural, as *wheat, hay, copper, sugar, broth.*

CHAPTER IV.

SUBSTANTIVES.—GENDER.

§ 7. GENDER is the word used in grammar for sex. Nouns which denote male sex are said to be of MASCULINE GENDER. Nouns which are of female sex are said to be of FEMININE GENDER. Those which are neither male nor female are said to be of NEUTER GENDER.

Thus *man* and *John* are masculine, because they are names of male persons *woman* and *Susan* are feminine, because they are names of female persons; *sword* and *field* are neuter, because they are names of things.

Creatures, which are not persons, are frequently spoken of as things. They are then considered neuter.

§ 8. There are methods of pointing out gender in some cases.

i. Different words are used for the male and the female. For example:—

Masculine.	*Feminine.*
son	daughter
boy	girl
father	mother
bull	cow
ram	ewe

ii. Different endings mark the sex; *er* or *or* is most common for the masculine, and *ess* or sometimes *trix* for the feminine. For example:—

Masculine.	*Feminine.*
actor	actress
emperor	empress
master	mistress
widower	widow
testator	testatrix

iii. A word marking the sex is joined with the common noun. For example:—

cock-sparrow	hen-sparrow
he-goat	she-goat
man-servant	maid-servant

CHAPTER V.

SUBSTANTIVES.—CASE.

§ 9. If I say, "Thomas took John's book," I point out three Cases of Nouns substantive.

1. *Thomas* Nominative Case.
2. *John's* Possessive Case.
3. *Book* Objective Case.

The nominative and objective cases of nouns substantive are the same in form.

The possessive case is known by the ending *'s*. The mark (') is called *apostrophe*[1]. Sometimes, if the word ends in *s* or *x*, the apostrophe only is put after the last letter, as "in Felix' room."

In the plural of the possessive case the apostrophe is put after the *s*, as "for these things' sake," unless the plural ends in *en*, when *s* is added, and an apostrophe put before *s*, as "the children's bread."

[1] *Apostrophe*, derived from a Greek word, signifying *turning away*. The apostrophe is also used to mark the omission of a letter or letters, as *'tis* for *it is; tho'* for *though*. The old form of the possessive ended in *—es*, as book, poss. *bookes*. Hence the apostrophe in book's shows the omission of *e*. It seems to have been a mistake as to this apostrophe which led some old writers to use the pronoun *his* for *'s*, as *Asa his heart* for *Asa's heart*. And so in our Liturgy we have *for Jesus Christ his sake*, instead of *for Jesus Christ's sake*. This use of *his* is now obsolete.

The following instances show the cases of nouns substantive:—

	Sing.	*Plur.*	*Sing.*	*Plur.*
Nom.	book	books	man	men
Poss.	book's	books'	man's	men's
Obj.	book	books	man	men

Nouns are said to be *declined* according to the changes in the ending for the cases in the singular and plural numbers.

CHAPTER VI.

ADJECTIVES.

§ 10. NOUNS Adjective, or ADJECTIVES, are words added to substantives to express qualities belonging to them, as *dear* meat, *green* tree, *honest* man.

Adjectives have in general neither gender, case, nor number. We say "*good* king," and also "*good* queen," "*honest* man," and "*honest* men," without any difference in the form of the adjectives.

§ 11. Some adjectives are made into

substantives of the plural number by adding a final *s*, as *the blacks* for *the black men.*

§ 12. Adjectives have three degrees of comparison:—

1) The simple form, as *great, valuable, beautiful,* is called the POSITIVE form.

2) The COMPARATIVE is formed by adding *er* to the positive, as *greater,* or by using *more* before it, as *more beautiful.*

3) The SUPERLATIVE is formed by adding *est* to the positive, as *greatest,* or by using *most* before it, as *most beautiful.*

The second method is more common with the longer words, and the first with those that are shorter. We say *greater, greatest;* but we say *more beautiful, most beautiful.*

Adjectives ending in *e* make the comparative by adding *r*, and the superlative by adding *st*. The *er* and *est* form additional syllables, as fine, *finer, finest;* handsome, *handsomer, handsomest.*

Adjectives ending in *y* with a vowel before it add *er* and *est* for the comparative and superlative, as gay, *gay-er*, *gay-est*; but if a consonant come before the *y*, the *y* is changed into *i* before *er* and *est*, as happy, *happi-er*, *happi-est*.

Adjectives ending in a single consonant, preceded by a single vowel, double the consonant in the comparative and superlative, as fit, *fitter*, *fittest*; wet, *wetter*, *wettest*; fat, *fatter*, *fattest*; hot, *hotter*, *hottest*.

§ 13. Some words have no comparative forms of their own, but supply their want from other words which are not now in use. Thus:—

Pos.	*Comp.*	*Superl.*
good	better	best
bad, ill, evil	worse	worst
little	less	least
much, many	more	most

Some adjectives have two forms of comparatives and superlatives:—

far	farther	farthest
	further	furthest
old	older	oldest
	elder	eldest

CHAPTER VII.

NUMERALS.

§ 14. NUMERALS are words of number. They are used like adjectives.

The numerals, *one*, *two*, *three*, &c., are called CARDINAL.

The numerals, *first*, *second*, *third*, &c., are called ORDINAL.

After *third* the ordinals are formed by adding *th* to the cardinal number, as *fourth*, *sixth*, &c., up to *twenty*. (There are some slight variations, as *fifth*, *ninth*, &c.) We then say *twenty-first*, *twenty-second*, &c., till we get to a *hundred*. We then say *hundred and first*, *hundred and second*, &c.

Numeral adverbs will be noticed in Chapter XI.

NUMERALS.

	Cardinal.	*Ordinal.*
1.	One	First
2.	Two	Second
3.	Three	Third
4.	Four	Fourth
5.	Five	Fifth
6.	Six	Sixth
7.	Seven	Seventh
8.	Eight	Eighth
9.	Nine	Ninth
10.	Ten	Tenth
11.	Eleven	Eleventh
12.	Twelve	Twelfth
13.	Thirteen	Thirteenth
14.	Fourteen	Fourteenth
15.	Fifteen	Fifteenth
16.	Sixteen	Sixteenth
17.	Seventeen	Seventeenth
18.	Eighteen	Eighteenth
19.	Nineteen	Nineteenth
20.	Twenty	Twentieth
21.	Twenty-one, &c.	Twenty-first, &c.
30.	Thirty	Thirtieth
40.	Forty	Fortieth

	Cardinal.	*Ordinal.*
50.	Fifty	Fiftieth
60.	Sixty	Sixtieth
70.	Seventy	Seventieth
80.	Eighty	Eightieth
90.	Ninety	Ninetieth
100.	Hundred	Hundredth
101.	One hundred and one, &c.	Hundred and first, &c.
1,000.	Thousand	Thousandth
1,001.	One thousand and one, &c.	Thousand and first, &c.
1,000,000.	A million	Millionth

CHAPTER VIII.

PRONOUNS.

§ 15. PRONOUNS are words used instead of nouns substantive.

By the help of pronouns we avoid the too frequent repetition of the same word.

Instead of saying, "John was called. When John came, John's father praised John," we say, "John was called. When *he* came, *his* father praised *him*."

Any word which may stand by itself to denote a person, place, or thing, without a substantive being expressed, is called a Pronoun.

All and *some* are pronouns, because they may stand for *all persons* and *some persons.*

Many such pronouns may also be used with a substantive, as *all men, some things.*

These are in fact adjectives which, being of frequent occurrence, have come to be used as pronouns.

Pronouns are of five sorts:—1. PERSONAL. 2. DEMONSTRATIVE. 3. RELATIVE. 4. INTERROGATIVE. 5. INDEFINITE.

I. PERSONAL PRONOUNS.

The personal pronouns mark (1) the person who speaks; (2) the person spoken to; or (3) the person or thing spoken of.

Thus, when it is said, that *Thomas went to School*—

If Thomas speaks of himself, he says, *I* went.

If another person speaks *to* Thomas, he says, *You* went.

If another person speaks *of* Thomas, he says, *He* went.

I is called the pronoun of the *first* person—the person who speaks.

You is called the pronoun of the *second* person—the person spoken to.

He is called a pronoun of the *third* person—the person spoken of.

The personal pronouns are thus declined :—

FIRST PERSON.

	Sing.	*Plur.*
Nom.	I	we
Poss.	my *or* mine	our *or* ours
Obj.	me	us

SECOND PERSON.

	Sing.	*Plur.*
Nom.	thou	you *or* ye
Poss.	thy *or* thine	your *or* yours
Obj.	thee	you

In some books (especially in poetry) *ye* is put for the objective; as *I tell ye;* but this usage is not correct.

Thou, thy, thee, are seldom used except in Scripture and in poetry; but in common language, although we are speaking of only one person, we say *you, your, yours.*

Ye always refers to more than one person. It is chiefly used in Scripture and in poetry.

THIRD PERSON.

	Sing.			*Plur.*
	Mas.	*Fem.*	*Neut.*	*of all genders.*
Nom.	he	she	it	they
Poss.	his	her *or* hers	its	their *or* theirs
Obj.	him	her	it	them

He and *she* properly refer to persons; *it* to things.

If we speak of what is not a person, but is an animal, as, the *horse,* we may say *he;* or if we speak of the *cow,* we may say *she:* but in both cases we may also say *it.*

If we speak of what is not an animal, as the *field,* or the *tree,* we must say *it.*

In Scripture, and in old writers, we sometimes find *his* applied to things, as: "Put up thy sword in *his* place." Matt. xxvi. 52. But this usage is not allowable now. The only way in which *he* or *she* can be applied to things, is when in a lively manner we speak of them as persons. As if in speaking of a ship we were to say, "She walks the waters like a thing of life." We are then said to *personify* the ship.

The possessive cases *my*, *our*, *thy*, *your*, *her*, *their*, are used in a different way from *mine*, *ours*, *thine*, *yours*, *hers*, *theirs*.

My, *our*, *thy*, *your*, *her*, *their*, *its*, are always joined with some substantive expressed, as "this is *my* house;" "that is *your* field."

Mine, *ours*, *thine*, *yours*, *hers*, *theirs*, are used without substantives expressed, as "this house is *mine*," "that field is *yours*." *His* is used in both ways.

Mine and *thine* are often used in Scripture language where we should now use *my, thy;* chiefly before words beginning with a vowel, as "*mine* own arm brought salvation."—*Isa.* lxiii. 5.

N.B. The words *his, hers, its, theirs,* are never written with an apostrophe before the last *s.*

The personal pronouns are all used as substantives.

II. DEMONSTRATIVE PRONOUNS.

§ 16. The words *this, that,* are called Demonstrative Pronouns, because they serve to *point out* persons or things, as "Look at *this,*" pointing to a near object; "Look at *that,*" pointing to an object farther off.

They are also used as adjectives, as *this book, that horse.*

They are formed thus:—

Sing.	*Plur.*	*Sing.*	*Plur.*
this	these	that	those

III. RELATIVE PRONOUNS.

§ 17. Words which refer, i. e. carry back

the mind to some person or thing mentioned before, are called RELATIVES. The word to which they refer is called the ANTECEDENT, as "the *man, who* came yesterday."—*Who* is relative to the antecedent *man*.

The pronouns *who, which*, are relatives.

Who is thus declined:—

Sing. and Plur.
Nom. who
Poss. whose
Obj. whom.

Which is nominative and objective of both numbers. It has no possessive case.

Who is used in speaking of persons only, and is never joined with a substantive. We never say, "who man," but "who—"

Which is generally used in speaking of things, and is used either with a substantive or without one, as "*which* thing ought not to be done;" "the hour is come *which* calls us home." But it is sometimes used in speaking of persons, as "Our Father, *which* art in heaven."

That is sometimes used as a relative, as "he *that* would live in peace and rest;" "mortals *that* would follow me."

What is used as a compound relative, and stands for *that which*.

Who, *which*, and *what* are often joined with *ever* and *soever*; *whoever*, *whichever*, *whatsoever*, and the like.

Whoso is sometimes used for *whosoever*.

IV. INTERROGATIVE PRONOUNS.

§ 18. *Who, which, what*, are used to ask questions, and are then called INTERROGATIVES.

Who speaks only of persons.

Which speaks both of persons and things.

What may be used with or without a substantive: with a substantive it applies either to persons or to things; without a substantive it speaks of things only. "*What* men are ye?" "*what* shall I do?"

V. INDEFINITE PRONOUNS.

§ 19. The following are called INDEFINITE Pronouns:—

any, all, each, either, neither, every, none, one, other, own, same, some, self.

Either means *one of two.* "*Either* of the three" is incorrect. We should say "*Any one* of the three."

Every, own, self are not used alone, but are combined with other pronouns. Thus *every one.*

Own is commonly added to the possessives of the personal pronouns, *my own, our own, their own,* and the like.

Self and its plural *selves* are often combined with the possessives of pronouns of the first and second person, *myself, yourselves, thyself, ourselves;* and with the objectives of the pronouns of the third person, *himself, herself, itself, themselves.*

These compound forms are used either as nominative or as objective cases.

One, *other*, are declined thus:—

	Sing.	*Plur.*	*Sing.*	*Plur.*
N. & O.	one	ones	other	others
Poss.	one's	ones'	other's	others'

When *other* is used as an adjective the plural is *other*, as *other men;* when it is used as a pronoun the plural is *others*. In Luke xxiii. 32, we read, "*two other, malefactors;*" but according to present usage we should have had *two others.*

Few, many, more, most, much, and some other such adjectives, are used as pronouns.

CHAPTER IX.

ARTICLES.

§ 20. The words *an, a,* and *the*, are called Articles. *An* means *one.* It is used before words beginning with a vowel, or with *h* silent, as *an ox, an ass, an hour, an ear.*

A is a shortened form of *an*, and is used before words beginning with a consonant, or with *h* sounded, as *a man*, *a horse*, *a year*.

An or *a* is called the INDEFINITE Article. It only tells us that *one* and no more is meant to be mentioned.

The is another form of *that*. It is called the DEFINITE Article. It tells us that a particular person or thing is pointed out.

CHAPTER X.

VERBS.

§ 21. VERBS are parts of speech which point out action (doing) or state (being).

Verbs are of two kinds.

i. COMMON Verbs, such as *run*, *hear*, *love*.

ii. AUXILIARY or helping Verbs, which are joined with some parts of common verbs to help to express varieties of time and manner.

The auxiliary verbs are *be*, *shall*, *will*, *have*, *may*, *can*, *must*, *do*, *let*.

Thus: "You *shall* hear a story." The verb *shall* joined with *hear* tells us that the time of hearing is not yet come, but is likely to come.

The verbs, *am*, *have*, *do*, *will*, *let*, are also used as common verbs, with the respective meanings, *exist*, *possess*, *perform*, *determine*, *allow*.

§ 22. When verbs express *doing* or *acting*, they are said to be in the ACTIVE VOICE, as *I beat*, *I have run*, *I shall stand*. When verbs express *being acted upon* they are said to be in the PASSIVE VOICE, as *I am beaten*, *I have been stopped*, *I shall be placed*.

§ 23. By means of their endings, or by the help of auxiliary verbs, verbs point out manner, time, number, and person.

i The word in grammar for manner is MOOD. There are five moods:—

1. The simple or indefinite form of the verb—the INFINITIVE Mood.

2. The mood for declaring or for asking questions—the INDICATIVE Mood.

3. The mood for command—the IMPERATIVE Mood.

4. The mood for stating a condition—the SUBJUNCTIVE or CONDITIONAL Mood.

5. The mood for stating actions which we have permission or power to do—the POTENTIAL Mood.

ii. TIME.—The word used in grammar for time is TENSE. Time is present, past, or future. *I walk* is PRESENT tense, marking time present. *I walked* is PAST tense, marking time past. Time future can only be pointed out by means of an auxiliary; *I shall love*, which is called FUTURE tense.

iii. NUMBER is sometimes pointed out by the ending. In the indicative mood, *thou walkest, he walks, thou walkedst,* are singular, *ye walk, they walk, ye walked,* are plural; but in the past tense the third person singular is the same as the plural, *he walked, they walked:* and the first person singular is always like the plural.

iv. PERSON.—In the indicative mood, present tense, the persons of the singular number are distinguished by their endings: 1. *I walk,* 2. *Thou walkest,* 3. *He walks.* In the past tense the first and third persons are alike: 1. *I walked,* 2. *Thou walkedst,* 3. *He walked.*

In the subjunctive mood the ending is the same for all persons and numbers. The form *wert* is an exception.

§ 24. Common Verbs are either TRANSITIVE OR INTRANSITIVE, i. e. they either carry on the action to another word, which is called the object; or the action which they express is complete in itself, and requires no object to be mentioned.

Thus: *beat* requires an object, to which the action must pass. It is therefore said to be TRANSITIVE.

Sleep requires no object, and is therefore INTRANSITIVE.

§ 25. A PARTICIPLE is a part of a verb which may be used as an adjective, or, in other words, it is an adjective partaking of the nature of a verb.

Most verbs have two participles belonging to them: 1. The participle in *ing*; 2. the participle in *d*, *t*, or *n*.

The participle in *ing* is of the present tense, and is in the active voice, whether transitive or intransitive, as *walking*, *sitting*, *running*. It is called the PRESENT PARTICIPLE.

The participle in *d*, *t*, or *n*, is of the past tense, and may be either in the active or passive voice. This is called the PAST PARTICIPLE.

The past participles of transitive verbs

are sometimes active and sometimes passive, as I have *beaten*, or I am *beaten*; I have *raised*, or I have been *raised*.

But the past participles of intransitive verbs are never passive. We say, I have *walked*, I have *slept*; but not, I am *walked*, I have been *slept*.

§ 26. The following are called the PRINCIPAL PARTS of verbs—1. the simple form, as *love, sit*: 2. the first person singular of the past tense, *loved, sat*: 3. the participle present, *loving, sitting*: 4. the participle past, *loved, sat*.

A verb is said to be *conjugated* when we go through its *voices, moods, tenses, persons*, and *numbers*.

§ 27. We will first conjugate the auxiliary verbs.

1. BE:—

There are three different verbs from which the several parts, as here given, come: *am*, of which there is in use only the indicative present; *was*, of which the past tenses, indicative and subjunctive, remain; and *be*, used in the infinitive and subjunctive present. In old writers we sometimes find *be* used in the indicative present: second person singular *thou beest*, and *be* in the plural of all persons.

INDICATIVE MOOD.

Present Tense.	*Past Tense.*
Sing. 1. I am	*Sing.* 1. I was
2. Thou art	2. Thou wast
3. He, *or* she, *or* it, is	3. He, *or* she, *or* it, was
Plur. 1. We are	*Plur.* 1. We were
2. You, *or* ye, are	2. You, *or* ye, were
3. They are	3. They were

IMPERATIVE MOOD.

Present Tense.

Sing. 1. ——	*Plur.* 1. Be we
2. Be thou	2. Be ye
3. ——	3. ——

SUBJUNCTIVE MOOD.

	Present Tense.		*Past Tense.*
Sing.	1. (if) I be	*Sing.*	1. (if) I were
	2. (if) Thou be		2. (if) Thou wert
	3. (if) He, *or* she, *or* it, be		3. (if) He, *or* she, *or* it, were
Plur.	1. (if) We be	*Plur.*	1. (if) We were
	2. (if) You, *or* ye, be		2. (if) You, *or* ye, were
	3. (if) They be		3. (if) They were

INF. MOOD, be. PART. PRES. being.
PART. PAST, been.

2. SHALL :—

INDICATIVE MOOD.

	Present Tense.		*Past Tense.*
Sing.	1. I shall	*Sing.*	1. I should
	2. Thou shalt		2. Thou shouldest
	3. He, *or* she, *or* it, shall		3. He, *or* she, *or* it, should
Plur.	1. We shall	*Plur.*	1. We should
	2. You, *or* ye, shall		2. You, *or* ye, should
	3. They shall		3. They should

3. WILL:—

INDICATIVE MOOD.

	Present Tense.		*Past Tense.*
Sing.	1. I will	*Sing.*	1. I would
	2. Thou wilt		2. Thou wouldest
	3. He, *or* she, *or* it, will		3. He, *or* she, *or* it, would
Plur.	1. We will	*Plur.*	1. We would
	2. You, *or* ye, will		2. You, *or* ye, would
	3. They will		3. They would

When *will* is used as a common verb, the second person singular is *thou willest*, and the third person singular *he wills* or *willeth*; and there is a present participle *willing*, and a past tense *willed.*

4. MAY:—

INDICATIVE MOOD.

	Present Tense.		*Past Tense.*
Sing.	1. I may	*Sing.*	1. I might
	2. Thou mayest		2. Thou mightest
	3. He, *or* she, *or* it, may		3. He, *or* she, *or* it, might
Plur.	1. We may	*Plur.*	1. We might
	2. You, *or* ye, may		2. You, *or* ye, might
	3. They may		3. They might

5. CAN :—

INDICATIVE MOOD.

	Present Tense.		*Past Tense.*
Sing.	1. I can	*Sing.*	1. I could
	2. Thou canst		2. Thou couldest
	3. He, *or* she, *or* it, can		3. He, *or* she, *or* it, could
Plur.	1. We can	*Plur.*	1. We could
	2. You, *or* ye, can		2. You, *or* ye, could
	3. They can		3. They could

6. MUST :—

INDICATIVE MOOD.

Present and Past Tense.

Sing.	1. I must	*Plur.*	1. We must
	2. Thou must		2. You, *or* ye, must
	3. He, *or* she, *or* it, must		3. They must

7. LET : This verb is used as an auxiliary only for the imperative mood, first and third persons : as, *let me go, let them go.* In all other moods and tenses, it is used as a common verb.

8. HAVE:—

INDICATIVE MOOD.

Present Tense.	*Past Tense.*
Sing. 1. I have	*Sing.* 1. I had
2. Thou hast	2. Thou hadst
3. He, *or* she, *or* it, has	3. He, *or* she, *or* it, had
Plur. 1. We have	*Plur.* 1. We had
2. You, *or* ye, have	2. You, *or* ye, had
3. They have	3. They had

IMPERATIVE MOOD.

Present Tense.

Sing. 1. ——	*Plur.* 1. ——
2. Have thou	2. Have ye
3. ——	3. ——

SUBJUNCTIVE MOOD.

Present Tense.

Sing. 1. (if) I have	*Plur.* 1. (if) We have
2. (if) Thou have	2. (if) You, *or* ye, have
3. (if) He, *or* she, *or* it, have	3. (if) They have

INF. MOOD, have. PART. PRES., having.
PART. PAST, had.

9. Do:—

INDICATIVE MOOD.

Present Tense.	*Past Tense.*
Sing. 1. I do	*Sing.* 1. I did
2. Thou dost	2. Thou didst
3. He, *or* she, *or* it, does	3. He, *or* she, *or* it, did
Plur. 1. We do	*Plur.* 1. We did
2. You, *or* ye, do	2. You, *or* ye, did
3. They do	3. They did

IMPERATIVE MOOD.

Present Tense.

Sing. 1. ——	*Plur.* 1. ——
2. Do thou	2. Do ye
3. ——	3. ——

SUBJUNCTIVE MOOD.

Present Tense.

Sing. 1. (if) I do	*Plur.* 1. (if) We do
2. (if) Thou do	2. (if) You, *or* ye, do
3. (if) He, *or* she, *or* it, do	3. (if) They do

INF. MOOD, do. PART. PRES., doing.
PART. PAST, done.

§ 28. Common verbs are thus conjugated:—

Simple form, LOVE.

INDICATIVE MOOD.

Present Tense.	*Past Tense.*
Sing. 1. I love	*Sing.* 1. I loved
2. Thou lovest	2. Thou lovedst
3. He loves	3. He loved
Plur. 1. We love	*Plur.* 1. We loved
2. You, *or* ye, love	2. You, *or* ye, loved
3. They love	3. They loved

IMPERATIVE MOOD.

Present Tense.

Sing. 1. ——	*Plur.* 1. ——
2. Love thou	2. Love ye
3. ——	3. ——

SUBJUNCTIVE MOOD.

Present Tense.

Sing. 1. (if) I love	*Plur.* 1. (if) We love
2. (if) Thou love	2. (if) You, *or* ye, love
3. (if) He love	3. (if) They love

INF. MOOD, love. PART. PRES., loving.

PART. PAST, loved.

§ 29. The third person singular of the present tense indicative sometimes ends in *th*, as *hath*, *doth*, *loveth*, especially in Scripture language.

We generally say, *you love* instead of *thou lovest* or *ye love*, whether we speak of the plural or the singular number.

§ 30. Those given above are the only real tenses and moods in English; but other varieties of time and manner are expressed by the help of the auxiliary verbs.

Tenses expressed without auxiliaries are called SIMPLE TENSES.

Tenses made up by means of auxiliaries are called COMPOUND TENSES.

The auxiliaries which are joined with the other verbs to express varieties of time are called AUXILIARIES of TENSE.

The auxiliaries which are joined with other verbs to express varieties of manner are called AUXILIARIES of MOOD.

The auxiliary verbs of TENSE are, *am*, *have*, *shall*, *will*.

The auxiliary verbs of MOOD are, *may*, *can*, *let*, *must*.

Remember that the present and past tenses of *must* are the same in form.

We thus have altogether the following moods and tenses:—

In the indicative mood six tenses.

1. The PRESENT. 2. The PAST. 3. The PERFECT, which expresses action complete. 4. The PLUPERFECT, which expresses action complete before a given time. 5. The FUTURE. 6. The FUTURE-PERFECT, which speaks of future actions as if they were complete.

By means of the auxiliary *do* we make what is called the *emphatic* forms of the present and past tenses. *I do love. I did love.*

Do is also used as an auxiliary without any special emphasis—1. In questions, *Do*

I say this? 2. In commands, *Do not say this.* 3. In negative assertions, *I do not say this.*

Don't, for *do not*, is more used in speaking than in writing.

The present participle of any verb, together with the auxiliary verb *am*, makes what is called the *definite* form for each tense, as *I am loving, I was loving, I shall be loving, I have been loving.*

In the imperative mood one tense—Present.

In the subjunctive mood two tenses—Present, and Past.

In the potential mood four tenses—Present, Past, Perfect, and Pluperfect.

In the infinitive mood two tenses—Present, and Perfect.

In participles three tenses—Present, Past, and Perfect.

The Passive Voice is formed throughout by a combination of the past participle with the different parts of the verb *be*.

§ 31. In the following table all the tenses, simple and compound, of the Active and of the Passive Voice are arranged side by side.

N.B. *The Teacher should accustom his pupils, when they are sufficiently advanced, to give an account of the several parts of each compound tense. Thus,* I will have loved, *the future-perfect of* love, *is made up of the indicative present of* will, *the infinitive present of* have, *and the past participle of* love. See Syntax, § 143.

In the imperative mood let *is itself always an imperative present, second person plural of the verb* let. Let me love, i.e. permit ye me to love. Let him love, i.e. permit ye him to love; *and so of the other persons.* Love *is here infinitive present following* let.

CONJUGATION OF THE VERB *LOVE*.

Principal parts — love, loved, loving, loved.

ACTIVE VOICE.	PASSIVE VOICE.
INDICATIVE MOOD.	INDICATIVE MOOD.
Present Tense.	*Present Tense.*
Sing. 1. I love	*Sing.* 1. I am loved
2. Thou lovest	2. Thou art loved
3. He loves	3. He is loved
Plur. 1. We love	*Plur.* 1. We are loved
2. You love	2. You are loved
3. They love	3. They are loved
Past Tense.	*Past Tense.*
S. 1. I loved	*S.* 1. I was loved
2. Thou lovedst	2. Thou wast loved
3. He loved	3. He was loved
P. 1. We loved	*P.* 1. We were loved
2. You loved	2. You were loved
3. They loved	3. They were loved

ACTIVE VOICE.	PASSIVE VOICE.
INDICATIVE MOOD.	INDICATIVE MOOD.
Perfect Tense.	*Perfect Tense.*
have	*have been*
S. 1. I have loved	*S.* 1. I have been loved
2. Thou hast loved	2. Thou hast been loved
3. He has loved	3. He has been loved
P. 1. We have loved	*P.* 1. We have been loved
2. You have loved	2. You have been loved
3. They have loved	3. They have been loved
Pluperfect Tense.	*Pluperfect Tense.*
had	*had been*
S. 1. I had loved	*S.* 1. I had been loved
2. Thou hadst loved	2. Thou hadst been loved
3. He had loved	3. He had been loved
P. 1. We had loved	*P.* 1. We had been loved
2. You had loved	2. You had been loved
3. They had loved	3. They had been loved

ACTIVE VOICE.	PASSIVE VOICE.
INDICATIVE MOOD.	INDICATIVE MOOD.
Future Tense[1].	*Future Tense.*
shall or *will*	*shall* or *will be*
S. 1. I shall love	*S.* 1. I shall be loved
2. Thou shalt love	2. Thou shalt be loved
3. He shall love	3. He shall be loved
P. 1. We shall love	*P.* 1. We shall be loved
2. You shall love	2. You shall be loved
3. They shall love	3. They shall be loved
Future-Perfect Tense.	*Future-Perfect Tense.*
shall or *will have*	*shall* or *will have been*
S. 1. I shall have loved	*S.* 1. I shall have been loved
2. Thou shalt have loved	2. Thou shalt have been loved
3. He shall have loved	3. He shall have been loved
P. 1. We shall have loved	*P.* 1. We shall have been loved
2. You shall have loved	2. You shall have been loved
3. They shall have loved	3. They shall have been loved

[1] In those tenses in which there are more than one auxiliary the teacher is recommended to exercise his pupils in conjugating the tense with each of the auxiliaries in turn.

ACTIVE VOICE.	PASSIVE VOICE.
IMPERATIVE MOOD.	IMPERATIVE MOOD.
Present Tense.	*Present Tense.*
S. 1. Let me love	*S.* 1. Let me be loved
2. Love thou	2. Be thou loved
3. Let him love	3. Let him be loved
P. 1. Let us love	*P.* 1. Let us be loved
2. Love ye	2. Be ye loved
3. Let them love	3. Let them be loved
SUBJUNCTIVE MOOD.	SUBJUNCTIVE MOOD.
Present Tense.	*Present Tense.*
S. 1. (if) I love	*S.* 1. (if) I be loved
2. (if) Thou love	2. (if) Thou beest loved
3. (if) He love	3. (if) He be loved
P. 1. (if) We love	*P.* 1. (if) We be loved
2. (if) You love	2. (if) You be loved
3. (if) They love	3. (if) They be loved

ACTIVE VOICE.	PASSIVE VOICE.
SUBJUNCTIVE MOOD.	SUBJUNCTIVE MOOD.
Past Tense.	*Past Tense.*
S. 1. (if) I loved	*S.* 1. (if) I were loved
2. (if) Thou loved	2. (if) Thou wert loved
3. (if) He loved	3. (if) He were loved
P. 1. (if) We loved	*P.* 1. (if) We were loved
2. (if) You loved	2. (if) You were loved
3. (if) They loved	3. (if) They were loved
POTENTIAL MOOD.	POTENTIAL MOOD.
Present Tense.	*Present Tense.*
may, can, or *must*	*may, can,* or *must be*
S. 1. I may love	*S.* 1. I may be loved
2. Thou mayest love	2. Thou mayest be loved
3. He may love	3. He may be loved
P. 1. We may love	*P.* 1. We may be loved
2. You may love	2. You may be loved
3. They may love	3. They may be loved

Active Voice.

Potential Mood.

Past Tense.

might, *could*, *would*, *should*, or *must*

S. 1. I might love
2. Thou mightest love
3. He might love

P. 1. We might love
2. You might love
3. They might love

Perfect Tense.

may, *can*, or *must have*

S. 1. I may have loved
2. Thou mayest have loved
3. He may have loved

P. 1. We may have loved
2. You may have loved
3. They may have loved

Passive Voice.

Potential Mood.

Past Tense.

might, *could*, *would*, *should*, or *must be*

S. 1. I might be loved
2. Thou mightest be loved.
3. He might be loved

P. 1. We might be loved
2. You might be loved
3. They might be loved

Perfect Tense.

may, *can*, or *must have been*

S. 1. I may have been loved
2. Thou mayest have been loved
3. He may have been loved

P. 1. We may have been loved
2. You may have been loved
3. They may have been loved

ACTIVE VOICE.	PASSIVE VOICE.
POTENTIAL MOOD.	POTENTIAL MOOD.
Pluperfect Tense.	*Pluperfect Tense.*
might, *could*, *would*, *should*, or *must have*	*might*, *could*, *would*, *should*, or *must have been*
S. 1. I might have loved	*S.* 1. I might have been loved
2. Thou mightest have loved	2. Thou mightest have been loved
3. He might have loved	3. He might have been loved
P. 1, We might have loved	*P.* 1. We might have been loved
2. You might have loved	2. You might have been loved
3. They might have loved	3. They might have been loved
INFINITIVE MOOD.	INFINITIVE MOOD.
Pres. Love, or to love	*Pres.* To be loved
Perf. To have loved	*Perf.* To have been loved
PARTICIPLES.	PARTICIPLES.
Present. Loving	*Present.* Being loved
Perfect. Having loved	*Perfect.* Having been loved

PAST PARTICIPLE.

Loved.

§ 32. Questions are asked by placing the nominative after the auxiliary verb, *Do I love? Am I loved?* or, when no auxiliary is used, after the common verb, as *Simon, sleepest thou?*

§ 33. When the future is used simply to foretel, it is as follows :—

Sing.	*Plur.*
1. I *shall* go	1. We *shall* go
2. Thou *wilt* go	2. You *will* go
3. He *will* go	3. They *will* go

"I or we *will* go" marks a deliberate choice on the part of those who go,

"thou, he
"you, they } *shall* go" marks that the persons who go have no choice in the matter.

In asking questions in the first and third persons, *shall* and *will* are used much as in making direct assertions. "*Shall* I hear the nightingale? *Will* he hear the nightingale?"

But in asking a question in the second

person, *shall* and not *will* is used in reference to an event simply future. "*Shall* you hear the nightingale? You *will* hear the nightingale; *shall* you not?"

Should and *would*, which are the past tenses of *shall* and *will*, are used in a similar manner, when we wish to make an assertion as simply conditional.

Sing.	*Plur.*
I *should* go	We *should* go
Thou *wouldest* go	You *would* go
He *would* go	They *would* go.

In asking questions, there is the same variety.

"If it were fine, I *should* go into the wood. You *would* hear the nightingale; *should* you not?"

When *should* and *would* follow *if*, there is no difference of usage in the different persons. "If I *should* go. If you *should* go."

See Syntax, § 141.

CONJUGATION.

§ 34. Verbs are said to differ in CONJUGATION according to the way in which they form their past tense.

There are two conjugations:—

1. When the past tense ends in *d*, *ed*, *de*, or *t*, as *loved*, *benefited*, *spelt*, *made*. This is called the REGULAR conjugation.

2. When the past tense is made by a change in the vowel sound of the verb, as break, *broke*; take, *took*. This is called the IRREGULAR conjugation.

The following are the chief irregular verbs. Many form their participles in *n*, *en*, or *ne*.

CLASS i. In which the vowel of the past tense is *a*.

Pres.	*Past.*	*Part.*
begin	began	begun
come	came	come

Pres.	*Past.*	*Part.*
drink	drank	drunk *or* drunken
eat	ate	eaten
give	gave	given
lie	lay	lain
ring	rang	rung
run	ran	run
see	saw	seen
shrink	shrank *or* shrunk	shrunk *or* shrunken
sing	sang	sung
sink	sank *or* sunk	sunk *or* sunken
sit	sat	sat
stink	stank *or* stunk	stunk
swim	swam	swum
spring	sprang *or* sprung	sprung

Class ii. In which the vowel is *e*.

blow	blew	blown
crow	crew	crowed
draw	drew	drawn

Pres.	*Past.*	*Part.*
fall	fell	fallen
fly	flew	flown
grow	grew	grown
hold	held	holden *or* held
know	knew	known
slay	slew	slain
throw	threw	thrown

CLASS iii. In which the vowel is *o*, *u*, or *ou*.

abide	abode	abode
bind	bound	bound
bear	bore *or* bare	borne
break	broke *or* brake	broken
choose	chose	chosen
cleave	clove *or* clave	cloven *or* cleft
cling	clung	clung
dig	dug	dug *or* digged
drive	drove	driven
fight	fought	fought
find	found	found

Pres.	*Past.*	*Part.*
fling	flung	flung
forsake	forsook	forsaken
freeze	froze	frozen
get	got	gotten *or* got
grind	ground	ground
hang	hung *or* hanged	hung *or* hanged
ride	rode	ridden
rise	rose	risen
shake	shook	shaken
shine	shone	shone
smite	smote	smitten
speak	spoke	spoken
spin	spun	spun
stand	stood	stood
steal	stole	stolen
stick	stuck	stuck
sting	stung	stung
stride	strode	strode *or* stridden
strike	struck	struck *or* stricken
string	strung	strung

Pres.	*Past.*	*Part.*
strive	strove	striven
swear	swore	sworn
swing	swung	swung
tear	tore	torn
take	took	taken
tread	trod	trodden
thrive	throve	thriven
wear	wore	worn
weave	wove	woven
win	won	won
wind	wound	wound
wring	wrung	wrung
write	wrote	written

CLASS IV. In which the vowel is *i*.

bite	bit	bitten *or* bit
chide	chid *or* chode	chidden *or* chid
do	did	done
hide	hid	hidden
slide	slid	slid

Some participles from regular verbs end in *n* or *en*.

Pres.	*Part.*	*Pres.*	*Part.*
lade	laden	sew	sewn
hew	hewn	sow	sown
melt	molten	show	shown
mow	mown	strew	strown
shave	shaven	swell	swollen
shear	shorn		

§ 35. Verbs which are wanting in certain principal parts are called DEFECTIVE.

Can, *shall*, *may*, have only the present and past tenses of the indicative mood.

Must was originally a past form, but is used as a present as well as a past tense.

Ought is the past tense of *owe*, but seems to be used as a present. See Syntax, § 145.

Methinks, *meseems*, are IMPERSONAL verbs, equivalent to *it appears to me*, *it seems to me*. The former has a past tense, *methought*.

CHAPTER XI.

PARTICLES.

PREPOSITIONS, CONJUNCTIONS, ADVERBS.

§ 36. PARTICLES are small parts of speech, used to join words or sentences to each other, or to qualify other words.

§ 37. PREPOSITIONS are particles placed before nouns, pronouns, verbs in the infinitive mood, or present participles, to point out time, place, or circumstance. Some prepositions are also used as adverbs.

The following are the prepositions most in use:—

of, for, by, with ; at, to, from ; in, into, towards ; on, upon, off ; through, beyond ; within, without ; under, over ; above, below, beneath ; against, about ; around, among, between ; before, behind ; during, after.

§ 38. CONJUNCTIONS are particles used to unite sentences together, or to express opposition between them.

The following are the conjunctions most in use:—

and, as; either, or, neither, nor; although, though, but, than; for, that, because; if, unless, lest.

Conjunctions which unite are called coupling, or COPULATIVE Conjunctions, as *and, as, also, for.*

Conjunctions which oppose are called ADVERSATIVE, as *but, although, either.*

§ 39. ADVERBS are particles used to qualify verbs, adjectives, or other adverbs.

Some of the most common adverbs are: *even, so, also, too; now, often, always, seldom, ever, never; very, rather.*

Adverbs are added to verbs to express either the time, or the place, or the manner of the action. "I speak *now.*" "He sat *here.*" "You come *slowly.*"

Adverbs are added to adjectives or other

adverbs to mark degree. "John is *very* good." "Jane reads *rather* slowly."

1. Many adverbs are the same in form as nouns adjective, as *far*, *near*, *ill*; and most adjectives may be made adverbs by adding *ly*, which means *like*; as *smooth-ly*, *plain-ly*.

2. Many adverbs are formed from pronouns; e. g.:—*thus*, *here*, *there*, *hence*, *thence*, *hither*, *thither*, *then*.

Of these *here*, *hence*, *hither* refer to a near place; *there*, *thence*, *thither* to a place more remote.

The relative and interrogative adverbs are formed in the same way:—*how*, *where*, *whence*, *whither*, *when*, *why*, *wherefore*.

Relative adverbs also perform the part of conjunctions.

The adverbs *here*, *there*, and *where* are often combined with the prepositions *of*, *by*, *in*, *&c.*—

hereof, i.e. *of this* matter; *hereby*, i. e. *by this* thing; *herein*, i.e. *in this* place;

thereof, i.e. *of that* matter; *whereof*, i.e. *of which; whereby*, i.e. *by which*, *wherefore*, i.e. *for which*, and the like.

3. Numeral adverbs—*once, twice, thrice; firstly, secondly*, &c.

4. The adverbs *yes, yea, ay, no, nay*, are used simply to affirm or deny, without being attached to any other word.

Prepositions with substantives, with pronouns, or with adjectives are sometimes used as adverbs—

at length, at all, at least, at most, at first, at last, to-day, to-morrow, in earnest.

Hence come such adverbs as *indeed, along, abroad, aback, aright, away.* *a* is a shortened form of the preposition *on* [1].

[1] In Acts xiii. 36 we have *David fell on sleep*, exactly equivalent to the more common expression *fell asleep*. There is a similar contraction in the phrase *what's o'clock?* i.e. *what* is on the *clock?* (what hour is marked upon the clock.)

Some adverbs admit of comparison:—

much	more	most
near	nearer	next
soon	sooner	soonest

Adverbs in *ly* generally take *more* and *most*, as

more plainly, most plainly.

§ 40. INTERJECTIONS are words of exclamation, expressing surprise, joy, grief, &c., as *oh! alas! hollo!*

They are generally followed by the mark (!), which is called a note of admiration.

PART II. SYNTAX.

The beginner is recommended to confine his attention to those parts of the Syntax which refer to the Rules summed up in Chap. XVII.

CHAPTER I.

SUBJECT, PREDICATE, AND COPULA.

§ 41. SYNTAX is that part of Grammar which teaches us how to put words together.

A SENTENCE is such a collection of words as makes up a complete statement.

A sentence must always contain a verb expressed or implied.

SENTENCES are either SIMPLE or COMPOUND.

A COMPOUND SENTENCE consists of more than one SIMPLE SENTENCE.

In a compound sentence one simple sentence is often dependent upon another.

A CLAUSE is a simple sentence, which forms part of a compound sentence.

A PHRASE is a collection of words expressing some one idea, but not forming a sentence.

John was a good boy, and he was so industrious at school, that he gained a prize.

This is a compound sentence made up of three simple sentences, *John was a good boy, he was industrious at school* and *he gained a prize.*

The sentence *he gained a prize* is dependent upon the sentence *he was industrious at school.*

John was a good boy is a clause.

John, the most industrious of scholars, gained a prize.

The most industrious of scholars is a phrase. There is only a simple sentence here, which tells us that *John gained a prize.*

§ 42. A sentence fully stated consists of three parts; as, *John is good.*

1. The SUBJECT, the person or thing spoken of—*John.*

2. The PREDICATE, what is said of the subject—*good.*

3. The COPULA, which unites the subject and predicate—*is.*

The copula and predicate are often both contained in one word.

John runs.

Runs both tells us what is said, and that it is said of John.

The copula, when it stands by itself, is always some part of the verb *to be.*

§ 43. The subject of a simple sentence may either be the name of a person or thing, as *John, bread, virtue;* or a verb in the infinitive mood, as *To err is human;* or may consist of a word together with certain particulars belonging to it.

Such additions to a word are called ATTRIBUTES.

Strictly speaking the subject consists of the noun with its attributes; but it is usual to call the simple word the subject.

A well-known book of high character is a treasure.

Book is called the subject; *well-known* and *of high character* are called its attributes.

In the predicate too there may be attributes, as if we were to add to *treasure* the attribute *invaluable*.

A well-known book of high character is an invaluable treasure.

§ 44. If the verb be TRANSITIVE, there will be a person or thing to which the action passes. This is called the OBJECT of the verb.

God made the world.

The world is object of the verb *made*.

§ 45. There may also be words expressive of the manner, place, and time of action. These are called ADJUNCTS.

John passed William hastily in the street yesterday.

Hastily is an adjunct of manner; *in the street* is an adjunct of place; *yesterday* is an adjunct of time.

There may also be adjuncts of instrument and of cause.

I patted the pony with my hand.

With my hand is an adjunct of instrument.

I praised him for his gentleness.

For his gentleness is an adjunct of cause.

§ 46. The regular order of a sentence is Subject, Copula, and Predicate; but this order is often changed, especially in poetry.

Good is the word which he has spoken; i. e. The word which he has spoken is good.

CHAPTER II.

SYNTAX OF THE NOMINATIVE CASE.

§ 47. I. THE NOMINATIVE is the SUBJECT of some VERB.

I read. John runs. I and *John* are Nominatives.

§ 48. The subject is generally omitted when the verb is in the second person of the imperative mood.

Love thy neighbour. The subject is *thou* understood.

Obey your fathers. The subject is *you* or *ye* understood.

In Scripture and solemn speeches the Nominatives *thou* and *ye* are often expressed.

Go thou, and do likewise.

Speak ye every man the truth to his neighbour.

The Nominative is omitted in some common phrases.

Thank you, i. e. I *thank you. Pray,* i.e. I *pray. Prithee,* i. e. I *pray thee.*

In the phrases *as is said, as will be proved,* and the like, *it* is omitted.

King John, as has been said, was in London; i.e. *as* it *has been said.*

It refers to the statement of *King John being in London.*

§ 49. When the Nominative is far from its verb, a second Nominative is sometimes added.

They that go down in ships and occupy their business in great waters, these men see the works of the Lord.

They and *these men* are both Nominatives, subjects of the verb *see.*

§ 50. The Nominative sometimes has its verb omitted.

Thus far William, i. e. *thus far William* spoke.

Wherefore this haste? i. e. *whence* is *this haste?*

How beautiful the night! i. e. is *the night.*

Strange folly! i. e. is the *folly.*

Lo, a voice from heaven, i. e. came *from heaven.*

This omission is common in compound sentences, a verb being understood from a former clause.

We run as fast as they, i. e. *as they* run.

§ 51. In direct assertions the Nominative usually stands before the verb.

The nightingale will sing.

It sometimes follows the verb when the sentence begins with a particle or with an adjunct.

Then went the captain with the officers.

In those days came John the Baptist.

The particle *there* often stands before the verb to show that the Nominative will follow it.

Then there arose certain of the synagogue.

There was heard a sound of thunder.

The Nominative follows the verb in the phrases *said he, spake John, quoth I*, and the like.

The regular order of the Nominative and verb is often changed in poetry. See § 65.

§ 52. In interrogative sentences the Nominative follows the verb or the auxiliary.

In Scripture and in poetry the personal pronouns sometimes follow the simple forms of the present and past tenses.

Believest thou this? Saw they the man?

In common language the emphatic forms (see p. 55) of the present and past are used, and the Nominative follows *do* or *did.*

Do you believe? Did they see the man?

In compound tenses the Nominative stands next to the first auxiliary, unless it is separated from it by *not.*

Will Harry come? Will not Harry come?
Might John have been asked? Might not John have been asked?

§ 53. II. The NOMINATIVE is used after the verb *to be*, or its participles.

I am he. I is subject of *am; he* is Nominative following *am* and referring to the same person as *I.*

William has been a teacher. William and *teacher* are both Nominatives, and both refer to the same person.

The regular order of the words is sometimes inverted, especially in poetry.

King Edward was a warrior brave,
A warrior brave was he.

The regular order of the last verse would be, *He was a brave warrior.*

Such expressions as *It is me, It is him,* are incorrect.

The Nominative is used in the same way after *become, seem,* and the like, and after passive verbs.

She became queen. He seemed a gentleman.
Cicero was called the father of his country.

Queen, gentleman, and *father* are Nominatives.

It will be observed that every passive form is made up of some part of the auxiliary *to be,* and a past participle.

If the substantive following a passive verb do not refer to the subject of the verb, it is not in the Nominative. See § 65.

In the phrase *It becomes him, becomes* is used in a peculiar sense for *suits.*

§ 54. III. The NOMINATIVE is used in APPOSITION.

When two substantives, or a personal pronoun and substantive stand together, and both refer to the same person or thing, they are said to be in APPOSITION, and are always in the same case.

I the king decree.

John the Baptist came preaching.

I and *the king* are Nominatives in Apposition; *John* and *the Baptist* are Nominatives in Apposition.

Mister William Johnson is here.

Mister (usually written *Mr.*) *William* and *Johnson* are Nominatives in Apposition.

§ 55. IV. The NOMINATIVE is used with a PARTICIPLE, no verb being expressed or understood.

This is called the NOMINATIVE ABSOLUTE.

He being the first in his class, the other children looked up to him.

He is Nominative Absolute used with *being.*

The king having spoken, the prisoner was
led away.

The king is Nominative Absolute, used with *having spoken.*

The bow well bent and smart the spring,
Vice seems already slain.

Bow is used with the participle *bent,* but in prose *being* would have been inserted.

The bow being *well bent, and* the spring being *smart.*

Sometimes the Nominative stands by itself without a participle.

So down he came—for loss of time,
Although it grieved him sore,
Yet loss of pence, he knew full well,
Would trouble him much more.

Here *loss* (*of time*) is Nominative Absolute.

This arises from a change made by the writer in the form of his sentence. He begins as if he would write *loss of time would trouble him much* less than *loss of pence;* but as he goes on, he changes the form of his sentence.

§ 56. V. The NOMINATIVE is used when a person is spoken to.

Thy name, O Cæsar, is famous.

I am not mad, most noble Festus.

Love righteousness, ye that be judges of the earth.

Cæsar, Festus, and *ye* are Nominatives.

The Nominative is also used in exclamations.

O! the depth of the riches both of the wisdom and knowledge of God!

Depth is Nominative.

CHAPTER III.

GOVERNMENT OF SUBSTANTIVES.

§ 57. WHEN the case of a substantive depends upon another word, it is said to be GOVERNED by that word.

John's hat; like me; he saw thee; for him.

John's is governed by the substantive *hat*; *me* is governed by the adjective *like*; *thee* is governed by the verb *saw*; *him* is governed by the preposition *for*.

SYNTAX OF THE POSSESSIVE CASE.

§ 58. I. The POSSESSIVE is governed by a SUBSTANTIVE, and marks the person or thing to which that substantive belongs.

The queen's crown. The subjects' prosperity.

Queen's is governed by *crown*; *subjects'* is governed by *prosperity*.

§ 59. The substantive which governs the Possessive is sometimes omitted:—

1. When the Possessive forms the predicate of the sentence.

This hat is John's, i. e. *John's* hat.

The field is the children's, i. e. *the children's* field.

The house is yours, i. e. *your* house.

2. When *house* or *place* are understood:—

He came to my father's, i. e. *my father's* house.

The phrases *St. Paul's*, i. e. cathedral; *St. Bartholomew's*, i. e. hospital, are examples of this usage.

3. When the substantive may be understood from what has gone before:—

Whose book is this? It is one of my father's, i. e. *one of my father's* books.

This stick is not one of mine.

Of governs *sticks* understood, and *mine* is governed by *sticks*.

As to the Possessive forms *mine, yours*, and the like, see Accidence, § 15.

§ 60. The Possessive stands before its substantive, but may be separated from it by an adjective or adjectives belonging to that substantive.

We saw John's father.

Father is governed by *saw*, and *John's* by *father*.

Susan's bright and smiling face.

Susan's is governed by *face;* of which *bright* and *smiling* are attributes.

§ 61. When two Possessives come together, and the second has no article, the first is governed by the second, and the second by the substantive which follows.

His sister's son.

His is governed by *sister's*, and *sister's* by *son*.

§ 62. II. The POSSESSIVE is used in APPOSITION.

When a personal pronoun and substantive are in Apposition, both are in the Possessive Case.

His, the farmer's wife.

His and *farmer's* are in Apposition, and both governed by *wife*.

This kind of Apposition is not common.

When two or more Possessives are in

Apposition, the last only takes the final 's.

William the Conqueror's son.

Mr. William Johnson's house.

The substantives in Apposition are treated as one word.

§ 63. When two substantives come together, and one is an attribute of the other, this is usually in the Possessive, but sometimes is not so.

The hall door, the schoolroom table, a mountain lamb, the mother country.

These are in fact compound substantives (see Accidence, § 4), and might be connected by a hyphen, but the two words are often printed or written distinct from each other.

CHAPTER IV

SYNTAX OF THE OBJECTIVE CASE.

§ 64. I. THE OBJECTIVE is governed by

some Transitive Verb, and marks the object of that verb.

Harry liked school.

School is the Objective, object of the verb *liked.*

The master praised him.

Him is the object of *praised.*

The Objective sometimes follows a passive verb.

They will be taught obedience. Obedience is the object of *will be taught.*

§ 65. The object in its regular order follows the verb.

John assisted me.

But when stress is laid upon the object, it often comes first.

The father I respected, the son I loved.

Me he restored, and him he hanged.

In poetry the regular order is often changed.

For saddle-tree scarce reached had he.

i. e. *He had scarce reached the saddle-tree.*

§ 66. When the object has preceded its verb, the Objective of the personal pronoun is sometimes added.

Strawberry-blossoms, one and all,
We must spare them.

Strawberry-blossoms is object to *spare*, *them* is a repeated object.

§ 67. Some verbs take two objects, the IMMEDIATE, and the more REMOTE.

My father gave the horse some hay.

Horse and *hay* are both objects of the verb *gave;* but *hay* is the Immediate object, the thing given; *horse* is the Remote object, that to which it was given.

But if it is said,

My father gave the horse away;

horse is here the Immediate object, the thing given.

§ 68. The Remote object may be more fully expressed by means of the preposition *to* or *for*.

My father gave some hay to the horse.

A personal pronoun is most commonly used as a Remote object.

Send us the books. Tell him a story.

John will lend you a slate.

William has built them a cottage.

The Remote object, when expressed by an Objective without a preposition, must stand next after the verb.

Give the mother the foal means *give the foal to the mother.*

Give the foal the mother means *give the mother to the foal.*

§ 69. II. The OBJECTIVE is used after some INTRANSITIVE VERBS when its meaning is akin to that of the verb.

They have slept their sleep. He went his way.

Sleep and *way* are Objectives used after, but not properly speaking objects of the verbs *slept, went.*

§ 70. III. The OBJECTIVE is governed

by the ADJECTIVE *like*, and by PREPOSITIONS.

His daughter is like him. She treated her like me.

Like is the only adjective which governs a case.

All prepositions govern the Objective.

Of me, to thee, for him, from us.

No one will listen to the music except me.

Except is a preposition followed by the objective *me*.

§ 71. IV. The OBJECTIVE is used in APPOSITION.

This usage is precisely the same as in the nominative, § 54.

God save Victoria, our gracious Queen.

Queen, *Victoria*, are Objectives in Apposition.

§ 72. V. The OBJECTIVE is used to MEASURE TIME or SPACE.

They continued to travel ten days, i. e. during *ten days*.

We have toiled all night, i.e. during *all night.*

October is thirty-one days long, i.e. lasts for *thirty-one days.*

The lake is two miles broad and ten miles long.

Two miles and *ten miles* are Objectives used to measure space.

§ 73. VI. The OBJECTIVE is used in certain EXCLAMATIONS:—

Ah me! Me miserable!

CHAPTER V.

AGREEMENT OR CONCORD.

§ 74. THERE is CONCORD OR AGREEMENT in GENDER, NUMBER, CASE, and PERSON.

Words AGREE in GENDER.

When we say *she,* speaking of a woman, *she* and *woman* agree in Gender, both being feminine.

Words AGREE in NUMBER.

This man; this and *man* agree in Number, both being singular.

Words AGREE in CASE.

His, the farmer's horse; his and *farmer's* are both possessive; they agree in Case.

Words AGREE in PERSON.

He walks; he and *walks* are both third persons; they agree in Person; they also agree in Number, for both are singular.

SYNTAX OF ADJECTIVES.

§ 75. I. An ADJECTIVE is used with some SUBSTANTIVE which it qualifies.

A good man, a good woman, good men, good things.

Adjectives do not vary in their endings; *good* applies to man, woman, or thing, one or many.

Sometimes there may be a doubt to which of two substantives an Adjective belongs.

A good farmer's horse may mean either *a horse belonging to a good farmer*, or *a good horse belonging to a farmer.*

In the former case *good* qualifies *farmer's*, in the latter case it qualifies *horse.*

The sense of the passage must determine which of the two is meant.

§ 76. Adjectives are used in the comparative and superlative to express the degree in which various objects possess a certain quality.

John is good. William is better. Richard is best.

William is better when compared with *John. Richard is best* when compared both with *John* and *William.*

The comparative is used when only two objects are compared together.

This is the prettier of the two cats.

When more than two objects are compared the superlative is used.

Charles is the youngest of all the scholars.

Hence if there are two brothers we say

Which is the taller? if there are more than two, we say *Which is the tallest?*

In either case we may use the comparative with *than.*

Charles is taller than his brother.

Or, *Charles is taller than his brothers.*

§ 77. Double comparatives and superlatives are improper.

It is incorrect to say *more braver* or *worser* for *more brave* or *worse.*

We sometimes however find, even in good writers, *lesser* used for *less*, and in Acts xxvi. 5 we read *the most straitest sect.*

In Scripture the term *Most Highest* is applied to GOD, in order to express surpassing majesty.

Such words as *extreme, supreme,* since they express in themselves quality in a superlative degree, do not properly admit of comparison.

§ 78. An Adjective generally stands before its substantive, but sometimes, especially in poetry, follows it.

I am a linendraper bold.

When there are adjuncts belonging to the Adjective, it follows the substantive.

The moon, lovely in her brightness, gladdens the night.

§ 79. II. An ADJECTIVE stands alone after the verbs *am*, *become*, and the like, or their participles.

Cæsar was ambitious.

The men becoming brave.

§ 80. III. An ADJECTIVE with the DEFINITE ARTICLE has sometimes its substantive omitted but understood.

Which horse will you have? I will have the white, i. e. the white horse.

§ 81. The plural *men* is often understood.

Toll for the brave, i. e. *the brave* men.

Sometimes an Adjective is made into a plural substantive by the addition of *s*. See Accidence, § 11.

§ 82. The substantive belonging to an Adjective in the comparative or in the superlative is often omitted.

There hath not arisen a greater than John the Baptist, i. e. *a greater* man.

The wisest of the Athenians give them laws, i. e. *the wisest* men.

§ 83. IV. An ADJECTIVE with the DEFINITE ARTICLE is used to express an abstract quality.

Admire the beautiful, but love the good, i. e. *Admire* what is *beautiful, but love* what is *good.*

In the same way *the dark* is used for *darkness*, and the like.

§ 84. V. Some few ADJECTIVES are used like ADVERBS, as *right, wrong, fast*, and in the comparative and superlative degrees, *better, best, worse, worst.*

Have you done your sum right? No; I did it wrong. You did it too fast.

Right, wrong, fast, mark the manner of doing.

Right and *pretty* are used as adverbs of degree, e.g. *right well; pretty good.*

But generally such expressions as *the knife cuts* sharp, *the ball runs* smooth, are incorrect.

§ 85. All NUMERALS are Adjectives, and follow the same rules of Syntax.

Three children.

We are seven, i. e. *seven* persons.

§ 86. The Numerals stand alone when they express an abstract number.

Two and two make four.

CHAPTER VI.

SYNTAX OF PRONOUNS.

§ 87. PERSONAL Pronouns are used as substantives, and have been considered with them.

Relative and Interrogative Pronouns will be considered in the next chapter.

All other Pronouns partake of the nature of adjectives, and may be called ADJECTIVAL.

§ 88. I. ADJECTIVAL PRONOUNS are used with a SUBSTANTIVE expressed.

This girl, each bird, all persons.

Demonstrative Pronouns which vary according to their number must agree in number with the substantive to which they belong.

This boy, these boys; that man, those men.

In such phrases as *this ten years*, *ten years* is considered as one space of time, and *this* agrees with *space* implied in *ten years*.

§ 89. II. ADJECTIVAL PRONOUNS stand alone, but some substantive is understood.

This, standing by itself, may refer to any person or thing. The particular sentence determines to what substantive it belongs.

If you admire a watch, look at this, i.e. *this* watch.

Each has her own task.

If we have been speaking of *women*, it is *each woman*; if we speak of *bees*, it is *each bee*.

Here, said one, is your hatchet, i.e. *one* person.

The one, the other are used to mark a person, thing, or class, as opposed to another person, thing, or class.

Cimon and Pericles were rival statesmen; the one courted the nobles, the other flattered the people.

The one man, viz. *Cimon*, is opposed to *the other* man, viz. *Pericles*.

Of these tables the one is mine, the other is yours.

A meeting differs from a mob, the one being orderly, the other turbulent.

§ 90. Adjectival Pronouns do not in general take an article; *one, other*, and *same* are exceptions.

Such an one, another, the one, the other, the same.

CHAPTER VII.

SYNTAX OF THE RELATIVE AND INTERROGATIVE PRONOUNS.

§ 91. I. A RELATIVE PRONOUN agrees with its ANTECEDENT in GENDER and NUMBER, but not in CASE.

Who, whose, whom are either singular or plural, masculine or feminine, but not neuter; *which* is singular or plural, and generally neuter.

He, who knows his lesson may repeat it.

Who is masculine singular, agreeing with its Antecedent *he* in gender and number. *Who* and *he* are both nominatives, but from independent causes, for if we changed *he* into *him* we should still say *who: Let him who knows his lesson repeat it.*

I spoke to the women, whose husbands you mentioned.

Whose is feminine plural, agreeing with *women* in gender and number; but *women* is objective, and *whose* is possessive.

That is the horse which he saw at the fair.

Which is neuter singular, agreeing with its Antecedent *horse* in gender and number; but *horse* is nominative, and *which* is objective.

The soldiers appeared, which frightened the rebels.

The Antecedent of *which* is *thing* (viz. the appearing of the soldiers) implied in the previous clause.

Who is used of all persons, *I who am, Thou who art, He who is, We who are*, and the like.

Our Father, which art in heaven.

Here *which* is masculine (see Accidence, § 17), and is second person singular, referring to its Antecedent *Thou* understood.

Who, whose, whom are not properly applied to things. They are sometimes applied to *animals*, because animals may be spoken of as *persons*. See Accidence, p. 33.

§ 92. *Which* is sometimes accompanied by a substantive denoting either a person or a thing, when we wish to mark particularly to what the Relative belongs.

At which day. With all which kings and states.

Who, whose, and *whom* are not used in this manner.

§ 93. The Antecedent is sometimes omitted.

Who steals my purse, steals trash.

The Antecedent of *who* is *he* understood.

Vengeance strikes whom Heaven decrees to fall.

The Antecedent of *whom* is *him* understood.

§ 94. II. The CASE of a RELATIVE PRONOUN depends upon the sentence to which it belongs.

He who knows his lesson may repeat it.

Who is nominative, subject of *knows*.

I spoke to the women, whose husbands you mentioned.

Whose is possessive, governed by *husbands*.

That is the horse which he saw at the fair.

Which is objective, object of *saw*.

§ 95. A Relative Pronoun generally stands at the beginning of the sentence to which it belongs.

The possessive *whose* may be preceded by a word governing the case on which it depends:—

Concerning whose report.

Concerning governs *report*, upon which *whose* depends.

§ 96. The objective of the Relative Pronoun may either precede or follow the preposition which governs it; but if the preposition follows, it must be placed after the word to which it joins the Pronoun.

Of whom we have spoken, or, *whom we have spoken of.*

§ 97. The objective of the Relative Pronoun is often omitted.

The person I spoke to answered for those he brought with him, i. e. *the person* whom *I spoke to answered for those* whom *he brought with him.*

The nominative is sometimes omitted in poetry, but not so commonly.

He never counted him a man
Would strike below the knee.

Or, who *would strike.*

§ 98. The Demonstrative Pronoun *that* is used as a Relative of all genders, numbers, and persons, but must always stand first in its own sentence.

I that speak, i. e. for *I* who *speak.*

The goods that are in the house, i. e. *the goods* which *are in the house.*

The person that I alluded to.

In poetry there is sometimes a change in the regular order.

'Tis like a spider's airy web
From every breath that flies;

for *that flies from every breath.*

Observe; we can place no governing word before *that*, used as a Relative.

We cannot say *the person* to that *I alluded*, for *the person* to whom *I alluded.*

In old writers *that* is used for *that which.*

To do always that is righteous in Thy sight, i.e. that which *is righteous.*

§ 99. The compound Relative *what* contains in it both Antecedent and Relative.

I hear what you say, i.e. that which *you say*: *that* is object of *hear*, and *which* is object of *say*.

When a preposition precedes *what*, it governs the Antecedent contained in it.

I speak of what I heard, i.e. *I speak of* that which *I heard.*

If the preposition belongs to the sentence following *what*, that sentence is to be regarded as an indirect question. See § 106.

§ 100. *Whoever, whosoever, whichever, whatever,* and the like often have the Antecedent omitted.

Whoever pleases may learn to write, i. e. any one who *pleases may learn to write.*

If the Relative sentence stands first, and the Antecedent is in a different case from the Relative, the personal pronoun must be inserted in the sentence to which the Antecedent belongs.

Whomever you send, I will admit,
Whoever comes, shall be admitted,

because the Relative and Antecedent are in the same case.

But

Whomever you send, he shall be admitted,
Whoever comes, I will admit him,

because the Relative and Antecedent are in different cases.

These are to be regarded as repeated nominatives or objectives, see §§ 49. 66.

Any one whom you send, he, &c.
Any one who comes, I will admit him.

In such phrases as *whoever it may be*, the Antecedent *any one* is understood.

I will give it to the best boy whoever it may be, i. e. *to* any one, who *may be* the best.

These Pronouns are governed in the same manner as *what*.

He would deserve a prize to whomever I should give it, but I will give it to whoever is best, i. e. *he would deserve a prize*, I mean any one *to* whom *I should give it, but I will give it* to any one *whoever is best.*

The first *to* governs the Relative *whom*, the second governs the implied Antecedent *any one.*

§ 101. Observe that the use of *who* and *whoever* for objective cases is incorrect, as, for instance,

Who did you speak to? should be, Whom *did you speak to?*

I will give it to whoever I choose, should be, *I will give it to* whomever *I choose.*

§ 102. *Whatever*, *whatsoever* sometimes occur, the rest of the sentence to which they belong being understood.

I wrong no person whatever, i.e. *whatever* he may be.

I can say nothing whatsoever against him, i.e. *whatsoever* it may be.

§ 103. A Relative Pronoun joins its own sentence to that to which the Antecedent belongs.

That is the horse which he saw.

Which joins the sentence *which he saw* to the sentence *that is the horse.*

The Relative sentence often qualifies a particular word.

He who knows his lesson, may repeat it.

Who knows his lesson qualifies or is an attribute of *he.*

In this case the Relative sentence follows next to the word it qualifies. For this reason the sentence to which the Antecedent belongs often follows the Relative sentence.

But in all cases the Relative is properly said to join the one sentence to the other. *Who* joins *who learns his lesson* to *he may repeat it.*

§ 104. The Relative is sometimes governed by a word in a subordinate clause of the sentence to which it is prefixed.

Which when the Apostles heard of, they rent their clothes. (Acts xiv. 14.)

Which is governed by *of* in the subordinate clause *when they heard of.*

It is, however, better to avoid such constructions. The sentence in the Acts might be expressed thus:—

And when the Apostles heard of it, they rent their clothes.

INTERROGATIVE PRONOUNS.

§ 105. III. INTERROGATIVE PRONOUNS have NO ANTECEDENT, but they are used in their own sentences LIKE THE RELATIVES, which are the same in form.

Who knows his lesson?

Whose husbands did you mention?

Whom did Heaven decree to fall?

§ 106. These are in fact shortened forms of the sentences,

Name him *who knows his lesson.*

Name those *whose husbands you mentioned.*

Name him *whom Heaven decreed to fall.*

Hence it is that what are in fact Relative Pronouns have come to be used as Interrogative.

Such sentences as the following are shortened in the same kind of way.

Tell me who has done this, i. e. *tell me* the name of him *who has done this.*

You are well aware whose fault it is, i.e. *you are well aware* of the name of him *whose fault it is.*

I know to what you allude, i. e. *I know* the name of the thing *to which you allude.*

These may be considered as indirect questions.

Observe the difference between *what*

used as a Compound Relative, and *what* used in an indirect question.

I know what you are telling me. Here *what* is a Compound Relative equivalent to *that which. I know* that which *you are telling me.* But *I know what you told him.* Here is an indirect question, *I know* what it is which *you told him.*

CHAPTER VIII.

SYNTAX OF THE ARTICLES.

§ 107. I. The Indefinite Article marks that there is a class, of which some one is taken.

A man, an elephant.

The Indefinite Article cannot generally be used with proper names.

When *a Cæsar, an Edward* is spoken of, it implies either that there are many *Cæsars* or *Edwards,* as *An Edward subdued*

Wales; or that there are many persons resembling *Cæsar* or *Edward* in some quality. *He was a Nestor in counsel, an Achilles in war.*

The Indefinite Article cannot be used with nouns that include the whole class which they name. We cannot say *a bread, a beer.* In such sentences as

This is a bread you will like,
I can recommend you a beer that will please you,

a bread, a beer are improperly used for *a* sort of *bread, a* sort of *beer.*

The phrases *an army, a multitude,* &c., imply that there are many *armies, multitudes,* and the like.

A few, a great many, point to a collection of individuals, *few* or *many;* there being many such collections, out of which one is taken.

An abstract noun cannot have the Indefinite Article when it denotes the whole quality which it names.

Virtue, *wisdom*, and the like, when spoken of in general, cannot have *a* before them.

A virtue or *a wisdom* implies that different kinds of *virtues* or *wisdoms* are thought of.

Virtue is rewarded, and vice punished.

Temperance is a virtue, which of all virtues most surely brings its own reward.

§ 108. II. The DEFINITE ARTICLE is used to distinguish its noun from some others of its class.

The man means either *the man* I have mentioned, or *the man* I am about to mention. In each case it denotes *some particular man* marked out from the rest of men.

The Definite Article may be used either with singular or plural nouns.

The eldest son of a baronet inherits the title, the younger sons have no title.

The person who is *eldest son of a baronet*

inherits the title, those who are *younger sons have no title.*

A substantive in the singular with the Definite Article often denotes a whole class.

The painter must study nature, i. e. *the* person who is a *painter.*

This sentence is the same in meaning as *Painters must study nature.*

A proper name does not in general admit of a Definite Article, because it belongs to one person alone.

The Cæsar means some one Cæsar distinguished from others of the same name.

§ 109. If a noun is sufficiently defined in itself it does not require the Definite Article.

We may either say, *Victoria, the Queen of England*; or, *Victoria, Queen of England*; because *Queen of England* is in itself definite.

§ 110. If a substantive have an adjective and an Article, the Article in general stands before the adjective.

A fine boy. The tall man.

A substantive when preceded by an adjectival pronoun, does not in general admit of an Article.

This boy. Some girls. Other men.

With *many*, *such*, and with any adjective accompanied by *so*, the article *a* follows the adjective.

Many a woman. Such a book. So good a horse.

The is used in the same way with *all*.

All the gentlemen.

Where two nouns are connected by *and*, or *or*, the Definite Article is often omitted before the latter noun.

The soldiers and sailors, i.e. *the soldiers and* the *sailors.*

The good or bad, i.e. *the good or* the *bad.*

CHAPTER IX.

SYNTAX OF THE VERB.

§ 111. I. A FINITE VERB, when USED TRANSITIVELY, has an OBJECT expressed or understood.

A *finite verb* is a Verb in any mood except the infinitive.

Thus, *I read a book. Read* is a transitive Verb, *book* being the object.

I read merely expresses the action of reading. Some object is implied, but not expressed. Most transitive Verbs can be used in this way.

Thus, *He loves, she draws, the clock strikes.*

§ 112. II. An INTRANSITIVE VERB has no OBJECT.

I walk, they run.

Some transitive Verbs are also used intransitively.

Thus, *I move*, i. e. *I move* myself, i. e. I am put in motion.

Observe that this use of the transitive Verb differs from the former.

When we say, *the gardener sweeps, the boy rolls*, we say of the boy that he performs the act of *rolling* some object which is implied, but not expressed.

But when we say, *the stone rolls*, we mean that it performs the act of *rolling*, no object being implied.

§ **113.** III. A VERB agrees with its SUBJECT in NUMBER and in PERSON.

I speak. Both *I* and *speak* are in the singular number and in the first person.

Thou speakest. She speaks. They speak.

§ **114.** When there are two or more subjects to the same Verb, the Verb is in the plural number.

John and Harry are coming.

In the sentence *John or Harry is coming*, *John* and *Harry* are not both subjects of the Verb, but either one or other is. Therefore the Verb is singular.

There is no difference of form in the several persons of the plural number.

We speak, you speak, they speak.

But it is plain that with *we* the Verb is in the first person; with *you*, in the second person; with *they*, in the third.

If one of the subjects be *I* the Verb is in the first person plural, because if instead of the subject we used a pronoun it would be *we*.

John and I are here. We are late.

But if *thou* or *you* be one of the subjects the Verb is in the second person plural, because if instead of the two subjects we used a pronoun it would be *you*.

You and John are here. You are late.

§ 115. If the subject be a noun of multitude the Verb may either be singular or plural, because we may think of a multitude as one whole or as many individuals.

This people draw near me with their mouth. (Isa. xxix. 13.)

This people draweth nigh unto me with their mouth. (Matt. xv. 8.)

If we use *people* for *persons*, it is considered as plural.

These people are my followers.

The word *number* may be used either with a plural or singular Verb.

A number of persons was assembled; or, *A number of persons were assembled.*

The former is more strictly correct; but the latter is more usual, probably because the plural *persons* comes so near the Verb.

So, *Great was the company of preachers;* but, *A great company of priests were obedient to the faith;* the plural Verb follows naturally after *priests.*

We cannot say, *A number of persons*

thinks, because in the act of *thinking* they must be considered as individuals.

§ 116. Some substantives, though plural in form, are often used as singular because they together express one thing.

Riches is a doubtful blessing.

Alms is a good gift to them who give it.

This news has delighted me.

The best means of acquiring knowledge is by industry.

But we can also say,

Riches are in the house.

These alms are useful.

Riches and *alms* are really substantives in the singular number ending in *s*. They have come to be used with a plural Verb because they *appear* to be plural.

We may say, too, *These means are the best;* but scarcely *these news*, although *means* and *news* are really plural in their formation.

Observe, *The wages of sin is death* is not to be explained in this way. Here the order of the words is changed (see § 46), the sentence meaning, *Death is the wages of sin.*

A whole sentence may be the subject of a finite Verb.

That these things are true is most certain.

The fact here said to be certain is *that these things are true.* This sentence is, therefore, the subject of *is.*

§ 117. If two substantives are used to speak of some one thing the Verb is in the singular.

Bread and milk is wholesome.

Violence and spoil is heard in her. (Jer. vi. 7.)

§ 118. The phrase *It is* is followed both by singular and plural nominatives.

It is my uncle.

It is the drunkards and the profane who disgrace a village.

The implied subject of the verb *is* is the fact *that the drunkards and the profane disgrace a village.*

CHAPTER X.

SYNTAX OF THE SUBJUNCTIVE MOOD.

§ 119. I. THE SUBJUNCTIVE MOOD is used in dependent sentences to express an UNCERTAIN EVENT.

If John come, tell him I am here.

The Subjunctive *come* marks the uncertainty of John's coming.

Hence the Subjunctive is used after the words *lest, unless, except, whatever, so,* in the sense of "provided that," and the like.

I am cautious, lest I be deceived.

Any one may speak, unless he have already spoken.

Ye shall not go forth hence, except your youngest brother come hither.

I care not, so it be well understood; i. e. provided that *it be well understood.*

§ 120. After the words *before* and *until* we either have the Indicative or the Subjunctive, according as the event is certain or uncertain.

Thus, Night, oft see me in thy pale career
Till civil-suited Morn appear.—Milton.

Appear is Subjunctive, because the occurrence is uncertain.

But, when Milton writes,

And young and old come forth to play
Till the livelong daylight fail,

accuracy of construction would seem to require *fails*, because the *playing* is directly asserted, and there is no uncertainty about the time of its continuance.

So in the use of *although*.

We do not say, *He loves me not, although he be my child;* but, *He loves me not, although he is my child*, because there is no doubt about his being the child of the person speaking.

I will forgive him, although he be guilty.

This implies the *guilt* to be doubtful.

§ 121. The Subjunctive also follows *grant* or *grant that.*

Grant this be so.—Milton.

But grant the plea, and let it stand for just,
That man make men his prey because he must.—Cowper.

Grant that this day we fall into no sin, neither run into any kind of danger.

Fall and *run* are Subjunctives.

§ 122. The Subjunctive sometimes follows *that* when it is put for *in order that*, but the auxiliary *may* is generally introduced.

Give us that due sense of all thy mercies, that our hearts may be unfeignedly thankful, and that we show forth thy praise, i. e. may *show*.

§ 123. The indicative is sometimes used even when the event is uncertain, the uncertainty being marked by the conjunction.

If he shows them not to you at first, do not believe that they are less powerful.—Sir W. Scott.

If a course of action is good, it needs no

vindication from the actor's motive; if bad, it derives none.—Sir W. Scott.

The indicative is seldom so used by older writers, and is less proper than the Subjunctive; but in the ordinary language of the present day the indicative often takes the place of the Subjunctive.

If John comes, tell him I am here.

If he was innocent, he would be acquitted.

If he were innocent would be more correct.

§ 124. *If* is sometimes omitted, and the uncertainty expressed by the verb in the Subjunctive followed by the nominative.

Were this so, I would go away.

§ 125. II. The SUBJUNCTIVE is used to express a CONDITIONAL EVENT. Thus *were* is used for *would be.*

Better it were that there were none at all; i. e. *It* would be *better* if there were *none at all.*

§ 126. III. The SUBJUNCTIVE is used to

supply the place of the third person of the IMPERATIVE mood.

Be it so, i. e. let *it be so.*

Thy kingdom come, i. e. let *Thy kingdom come.*

And, as I wake, sweet music breathe
Above, around, or underneath.—Milton.
i. e. let *sweet music breathe.*

CHAPTER XI.

SYNTAX OF THE INFINITIVE MOOD.

§ 127 A VERB in the INFINITIVE MOOD is used as a SUBSTANTIVE. It commonly follows the preposition *to.*

Either *love* or *to love* is called the Infinitive of the verb *love;* but, strictly speaking, *to love* is the Infinitive together with the preposition *to.*

§ 128. I. The INFINITIVE with *to* may be the SUBJECT of a finite verb.

To err is human, to forgive divine.

To err is Infinitive, subject of *is*; and *to forgive* is subject of *is* understood.

§ 129. II. When ONE VERB FOLLOWS ANOTHER it is in the INFINITIVE.

The Infinitive is without *to* after the auxiliaries *do, will, shall, may, can, must,* and *let.*

> *I shall speak. I may speak. Let me speak. I do believe.*

Hence we learn that the compound tenses, in which these auxiliaries are used, are made up of two verbs.

I would love is made up of *would*, the past tense indicative of *will*, and *love*, which is present Infinitive.

Also after the verbs *see, hear, feel, bid, need.*

> *I saw him rise. I heard him speak. I felt you touch me. I bid you go. I need not stay.*

Also after the verbs *have* and *dare* in certain cases.

I would have you speak when you are

spoken to, i. e. *I would* wish you *to speak.*

But *I have to speak*, i. e. *I* am obliged *to speak.*

I dare say, i. e. *I* venture *to say.*

But *I dare you to speak*, i. e. *I* defy *you to speak.*

§ 130. The Infinitive in these cases is in fact the object of the verb which it follows.

I bid you speak. Speak is the thing bidden. *You* is the person *bidden.* Both are objects of *bid.*

The same is true of the auxiliary verbs, as may be shown in the case of *will.*

I will it. It is the object of will; the thing willed.

I will speak. Speak is the thing willed, and therefore the object of *will.*

§ 131. More than two verbs may be used together.

You shall hear me bid John see the man go. Hear, bid, see, go, are all Infinitives:

hear follows *shall; bid* follows *hear; see* follows *bid; go* follows *see.*

We must not suppose that in such expressions as *I think you see, see* is Infinitive. The sentences, *I think I see, I thought you saw,* show that *see* and *saw* are indicatives. The sentences are compound, the conjunction *that* being understood. *I think* that *you see, I think* that *I see, I thought* that *you saw.* See § 165.

§ 132. With other verbs, whether transitive or intransitive, the preposition *to* comes before the Infinitive.

I command you to depart, I wish you to speak, I go to explain.

§ 133. The Infinitive with *to* may also follow a substantive or an adjective.

There is a time to speak, and a time to be silent.

Ready to give, and glad to distribute.

The active Infinitive sometimes *seems* to be used for the passive.

These apples are not fit to eat.

All these uses of the Infinitive are easily explained by considering that it is used like a substantive with the preposition *to*.

I go to explain. *To* shows the relation of *explain* to *go*.

It is the act *to* which the *going* is directed.

There is a time to speak. *To* shows that *speak* refers to *time*.

Ready to give. *Give* is the action *to* which there is *readiness*.

These apples are not fit to eat. *Eating* is the act to which the *fitness* refers; there is a want of *fitness* in relation *to* persons' *eating* them, i. e. *it is not fit for* persons *to eat* them.

This might also be expressed by *They are not fit to be eaten*, and hence the active Infinitive *seems* to be, but is not really, used for the passive.

§ 134. III. The INFINITIVE, like the finite verb, may have its OBJECT and its ADJUNCTS.

You must study grammar. Grammar is object of the Infinitive *study.*

To depart from evil is wisdom. From evil is an adjunct of the Infinitive *to depart.*

CHAPTER XII.

THE USE OF THE TENSES.

§ 135. The Present tense is used of an action which takes place at the present time.

I tell you this. It rains.

If we wish to mark more definitely that the action is now going on, we use the present participle with the verb *am.*

I am telling you this. It is raining.

This is called the *definite* form of the Present because it marks the time definitely.

If we wish to assert a fact more positively we use the verb *do* with the infinitive.

I do tell you this. It does rain.

This is called the *emphatic* form because it asserts a fact *emphatically*.

§ 136. The Present is used in speaking of an action without any particular reference to time.

He writes fairly. The children behave well.

So with the adverbs *often, sometimes,* which denote an action performed more than once.

The master sometimes praises me. Children are often careless.

§ 137. The Present is used in speaking of past events when they are related in a lively manner.

Along the skies
Tossed and retossed, the ball incessant flies.
They sport, they feast, Nausicaa lifts her voice

And warbling sweet makes heaven and earth rejoice.—Pope.

This usage of the Present is most common in poetry. In Latin and in French it often occurs in historical narrative. The Present so used is called the *Historic Present.*

§ 138. The Past tense is used in speaking of a past action.

John came. William appeared.

The verb leaves the time indefinite, only marking that it is past. It may be defined by other words.

John came yesterday. William appeared at four o'clock.

If we wish to mark definitely that the action was going on at the past time referred to, we use the present participle with *was*, which is called the *definite* form of the Past tense.

I was reading yesterday. John was coming when it began to rain.

This tense is sometimes called the *Im-*

perfect, because it speaks of a past action not completed.

§ 139. When we speak of a past action as complete or perfected we use the past participle with *have*. This compound tense is for this reason called the Perfect.

Babylon has fallen. I have spoken.

There is also a definite form of the Perfect, which marks that the action has been going on during the time mentioned.

I have been speaking. It has been raining this morning.

§ 140. When we speak of an action which was complete at a past time we use the past participle with *had*.

John had come when William arrived.

The *coming of John* was complete at the time of *William's arrival*. This tense is called the Pluperfect; because the action is more than complete, it was complete some time ago.

There is also a definite form of the Pluperfect, as *had been coming*.

§ 141. The Future tense is used to express a future action. The Future can only be expressed in English by means of the auxiliaries *will* and *shall.* See Accidence, § 33.

Shall properly marks duty or necessity; *will* marks choice or determination.

If I simply foretel my own departure I speak of it as a thing in which my will is not considered. I *shall* go, or I *am to* go. But if I say I *will* go, I mark my will or determination.

If, however, I foretel the action of another person, I suppose that he acts from choice, and therefore I say Thou *wilt* go, He *will* go.

For if I say Thou *shalt* go, He *shall* go, I mark thát the person does not act of choice but of necessity.

This usage arises from the circumstance that when a person speaks of his own actions he does not bring forward his *will,* unless for some particular reason—but in speaking of other persons' actions he presumes that they act of free will, except in particular cases.

§ 142. When we speak of an action which will be complete at some future time we use the past participle with *will have* or *shall have.* This is called the Future Perfect tense.

I shall have finished my lessons at twelve o'clock.

There is also a definite form of the Future-Perfect, as *shall have been finishing.*

§ 143. Observe that the several parts of compound tenses may be considered separately.

I have loved. Have is indicative present of the verb *have,* and *loved* is past participle of *love.*

I shall have been loved. Shall is indicative present of *shall; have* is infinitive present of *have; been* is past participle of *be;* and *loved* is past participle of *love.*

It is incorrect to call *will love* or *have loved* present tenses. *Will* is a present tense of *will*, and *love* is infinitive of *love*; but the two together make up a Future tense of the verb *love*. They express the action of *love* to be performed at a future time.

In the same way *have loved*, although made up of a present tense and a past participle, expresses the action of *loving* complete or perfect, and is therefore properly called the Perfect tense of the verb *love*.

It must be remembered that the object is not the object of the verb *have*, nor of the participle, but of the Perfect made up by both.

Thus, *I have broken my stick*. *Stick* cannot be called the object of *have*, because then I should mean to say, *I possess my stick in a broken state*; nor can the participle *broken* without *have* be followed by an object. What I do mean is this, *I have completed the act of breaking my stick*, and *my stick* is object of the Perfect *have broken.*

§ 144. The tenses of what is called the Potential mood are all compound: the auxiliaries *may* and *can* being Present tenses, and *might, could, would*, and *should* Past tenses of the indicative mood. See § 129. This will in general explain the usage of the tenses of the Potential mood.

William may speak, i. e. is permitted to *speak. Then Joseph could not refrain himself*, i. e. was not able to *refrain himself.*

He might have been useful, i. e. was permitted to *have been useful.*

The usage of *would* and *should* in the different persons (§ 33) follows that of *will* and *shall.* See § 141.

§ 145. The Past tense of the Potential mood sometimes appears to refer to present time.

I could speak, but I forbear.

Here the power of speaking is considered

as past, because I do not intend to use it; as if I were to say,

I was about to speak, but I forbear.

Would is used in the same way.

I would gladly help you, but it is forbidden; i.e. I was willing *to help you*, but its being forbidden removes the will.

Similar to this are such expressions as

I would beg you to be quiet. You should be quiet.

Here, in order to express the wish or duty more gently, it is spoken of as past.

I was wishing to beg you to be quiet. You were bound to be quiet.

This explains the usage of *ought*, which is the past tense of *owe*.

Children ought to be obedient.

The obligation or duty is not really past, but the Past tense has come to be used from this method of putting a duty forward gently.

Would is also used to express an

uncertain event dependent on some condition.

You would go, if I told you to do so.

I could a tale unfold, whose lightest word
Would harrow up thy soul.—Shakspeare.

i.e. *Would harrow up thy soul,* if I unfolded it.

The case is put as a mere supposition, and the person who supposes must put the thing supposed before him as past. Suppose that *I unfolded the tale*, I may also suppose that *it was likely to harrow up your soul.*

§ 146. A wish may be expressed in different ways.

i. By means of the auxiliary *may* or *might* with the Nominative following.

May he prove a virtuous child!

Might I have this happiness!

The use of *may* is more common than that of *might.*

ii. By the phrases *Would that,* or *O that;* each of these being shortened forms of *I would that.*

Would that you were more careful!

O that we might live virtuous lives!

§ 147. Sentences joined together by conjunctions may be independent of each other.

John went, but Harry came.

The two events are evidently independent.

Sentences may also be introduced in different parts of the principal sentence, and yet be independent of that sentence.

He whom I saw yesterday is your brother, who will leave home to-morrow.

Here the sentences *whom I saw yesterday*, and *who will leave home to-morrow*, are introduced into the main sentence, but are not dependent on it.

The tenses in such cases are determined exactly as if each sentence was an independent statement.

§ 148. A sentence is dependent upon another when it makes no independent statement, but is introduced to qualify the action expressed by the principal verb.

The Subjunctive mood belongs especially to dependent sentences.

The auxiliaries *may*, *might*, *would*, and *should* are also commonly used in dependent sentences.

The Indicative mood frequently takes the place of the Subjunctive in such cases. See § 123.

§ 149. The tense of the verb in a dependent sentence varies with that of the verb in the principal sentence.

If it lightens, it thunders.

If it lightened, it thundered.

If it should lighten, it would thunder, or,

If it lightened, it would thunder.

If it should have lightened, it would have thundered.

Or (which is more common)

If it had lightened, it would have thundered.

If it lighten, it will thunder.

Where we remark that there is no Subjunctive Future; but the Subjunctive Present, expressing uncertainty, conveys in itself an idea of futurity.

Although *should* and *would* are really Past tenses, yet being used, as has been explained (§ 145), to express what is either Present or Future, we have such sentences as the following.

If it should lighten, it will thunder.

I should be obliged to you, if you will inform me.

§ 150. The action in the dependent sentence may be one which precedes that of the principal verb.

In this case observe, (1) that the Pluperfect has the same relation to the Past, and the Future-Perfect the same relation to the Future, which the Perfect has to the Present; and (2) that in dependent sentences the Perfect often takes the place of the Future-Perfect.

Then we have the following varieties—

I begin
or, *I have begun* } *after you have finished.*

I began
or, *I had begun* } *after you had finished.*

I will begin after you shall have finished.

Or, (which is more common,) *after you have finished.*

The verb in the dependent sentence is in the same tense whether the principal verb be Present, Future, or Perfect; and the same is true of the Past and Pluperfect.

When the dependent sentence expresses the purpose or end of the principal verb, and is therefore joined to it by some conjunction equivalent to *that* or *in order that*, we have the following rule:—

When the principal verb is Present, Future, or Perfect, the verb in the dependent sentence is Present; when the principal verb is **Past** or **Pluperfect**, the verb in the dependent sentence is **Past**.

I speak
or, *I shall speak* } *that you may obey.*
or, *I have spoken*

I spoke,
or, *I had spoken* } *that you might obey.*

CHAPTER XIII.

SYNTAX OF THE PARTICIPLES.

§ 151. I. PARTICIPLES, whether PRESENT or PAST, are used as ADJECTIVES.

A loving child. *A loved child.*

The Past Participle when so used is always passive.

A loved child means *A child who is loved.*

Hence the Past Participle of intransitive verbs cannot be used as an adjective.

We cannot say *a slept child.*

§ 152. II. The PRESENT PARTICIPLE of a transitive verb may be followed by an OBJECT.

I was buying a field.

An object sometimes accompanies a Present Participle when used as an adjective.

In this case the object is put before the Participle, with which it forms a compound word.

A money-getting people.

A self-loving generation.

§ 153. III. The PRESENT PARTICIPLE is often used as a SUBSTANTIVE.

Reading is a constant source of amusement.

Reading is used like a substantive in the nominative, subject of the verb *is*.

A Participle so used may govern the possessive, or be followed by an objective with *of*.

John's reading. A gathering together of the people. The blessing of Abraham.

The multitude of the wares of thy making. (Ezek. xxvii. 16.)

Where we observe that the Participle takes the article like any other substantive.

If there be no article, the Participle may govern a case, like the finite verb, and may have adjuncts.

You will find pleasure in reading books carefully. Books is object of *reading.*

They were three days in gathering spoils.

§ 154. The following instances of the use of the Present Participle deserve special notice:—

And the house, when it was in building, was built of stone . . . so that there was neither hammer nor ax nor any tool of iron heard in the house, while it was in building. (1 Kings vi. 7.)

Hence come such forms as *a-building; a* being a shortened form of *on* or *in.*

In the days of Noah, while the ark was a-preparing. (1 Pet. iii. 20.)

Such forms are now out of use: but to

this head are to be referred the phrases, *The house is building; the ark was preparing*, and the like: the preposition *on*, *in*, or *a* having been dropped.

We are not to refer these Present Participles to the intransitive use of the transitive verb (§ 112). For we cannot say, *this house builds, the ark prepared.* The usage is confined to the Present Participle.

It is clear that in (1 Kings vi. 7) and (1 Pet. iii. 20) a modern translator would have written, *the house when it was building; while it was building; while the ark was preparing.*

§ 155. IV. Some PRESENT PARTICIPLES are used like PREPOSITIONS. Such are *during, concerning, regarding, respecting, touching.*

John has been absent during the summer.

My husband spoke to me concerning that matter.

Of the use of the Present Participle with the nominative absolute, see § 55.

§ 156. V. The PAST PARTICIPLE, when used with the auxiliary *have*, has an ACTIVE sense.

He has slept. I might have spoken.

If the verb be transitive, an object and adjuncts may follow.

I might have spoken a word hastily.

The Past Participles of some intransitive verbs are used with the auxiliary *am*.

He is come, or *he has come*.

They are come, or *they have come*.

CHAPTER XIV.

SYNTAX OF PREPOSITIONS.

§ 157. I. A PREPOSITION is followed by a SUBSTANTIVE or some word used as a substantive.

Of John, for the brave, from me, to have, by loving.

Remember that the infinitive and present participles can follow Prepositions, because they are used as substantives. See §§ 127. 153.

§ 158. II. A PREPOSITION marks the RELATION of the WORD WHICH IT GOVERNS to SOME OTHER WORD in the sentence.

This may be instanced in the case of the Preposition *of*.

Of marks *derivation*; such a relation as the branch bears to its parent stem. *Of* differs from *from* in not implying separation; *a branch of a tree* may be remaining upon the tree, *a branch from a tree* must have been severed from it.

Hence *of* is equivalent to *belonging to*.

When *of* joins one substantive to another, it denotes that the latter is *derived from* or *belongs to* the former.

The son of William. The throne of the queen.

There may be more than one way in which one thing *belongs to* another.

Thus, *The care of the sheep* is *the care* belonging to or "exercised *towards*" *the sheep.*

The care of the shepherd is *the care* belonging to or "exercised *by*" *the shepherd.*

The sheep are the *object* of the care; *the shepherd* the *subject* who takes care.

In the latter case we may properly substitute the Possessive case, *the shepherd's care*, but not in the former.

In Isa. liii. 11, *by his knowledge my righteous servant shall justify many* is put for *by the knowledge* of him; but this is an unusual mode of expression.

The *love of God* may mean either *love* entertained *towards God*, or *love* entertained *by God. God's love* can only mean the latter.

Of with its substantive is used to express an attribute of the substantive to which it is joined.

A gentleman of worth, i. e. *a* worthy *gentleman*, one to whom *worth* belongs.

He is of age, i. e. a person of mature *age*.

Of often joins its substantive to a pronoun or adjective, of which the substantive is understood.

Some of them; which of us; the best of men, i. e. the *best* man *of men; seven of the eleven*, i. e. *seven* men *of the eleven* men.

The substantive governed by *of* denotes the class to which the pronoun or substantive belongs.

The phrase *all of us*, for *all we*, is sanctioned by usage, but is not, strictly speaking, correct; *all* and *us* referring to the same persons.

Of so used is sometimes called Partitive, because it denotes that there is a class of which *part* is taken.

The pronoun *some* is sometimes omitted.

We may eat of the fruit of the trees of the garden, i. e. *we may eat* some *of the fruit.*

Bravest of men means *braver than all*

other men, but it implies that this *bravest* belongs to the class *men*.

Hence we see that Milton's expression,

> *Adam, the goodliest man of men since born*
> *His sons, and fairest of her daughters Eve,*

for *Adam* goodlier than *his sons*, and *Eve* fairer than *her daughters*, is incorrect.

Of joins its substantive to an adjective or participle, the substantive being that which belongs to the quality described.

Fleet of foot, sure of hand, ashamed of the fault.

Of joins its substantive to a verb to denote that it belongs to the action described.

The room smells of violets.

The queen of her clemency pardoned him.

Of joins *clemency* to the verb *pardoned*. The *pardon* arose from *her clemency*.

Of with its substantive sometimes denotes the agent of the passive verb.

I am accused of the Jews, i. e. by *the Jews.* (Acts xxvi. 2.)

Of also joins its substantive to a verb in the sense of *concerning.*

I hear of this. You spoke of such things. He knows of this.

Observe, the Preposition *by* was in old times used in the sense of *concerning*, as we now use *of.*

In 1 Cor. iv. 4, *I know nothing by myself*, yet am I not hereby *justified, means I know nothing* concerning *myself*, i. e. I am not conscious of any wilful sin.

By is not now so used, but is put for *concerning* or *in regard to* in such phrases as *I will do my duty by him*, i. e. in regard to *him.*

§ 159. The various usages of each of the several Prepositions might be traced as in the case of *of.* It will be sufficient to note some of the principal relations which we express by means of Prepositions.

The relation of receiving—

He gave it to William. William is the receiver.

The relation of agent to the passive verb—

The house was built by John. John built the house.

Relations of place, time, instrument, cause, and manner of action—

1. *Place: to* London, *from* the country, *in* the house, *at* home, *on* the waggon.
2. *Time: at* midday, *from* morning *to* evening, *for* two hours, *in* a minute.
3. *Instrument: with* a spade.
4. *Cause: for* this deed.
5. *Manner: in* haste.

These Prepositions with their substantives make up what are called adjuncts of place, time, instrument, manner, and cause. See § 45.

Observe that the phrase *as to* is equivalent to *as referring to*, and *to* joins its substantive to the participle *referring* understood.

A Preposition is sometimes put before the adverbs *once, thence, hence, whence*: *at once* being equivalent to *at one time*; *from thence* (like *thence* by itself) being equivalent to *from that place*; and so of the rest.

On Prepositions used as adverbs, see § 172.

§ 160. The Prepositions stand before the words they govern, except in the case of the relative pronoun. See § 96.

CHAPTER XV.

SYNTAX OF CONJUNCTIONS.

§ 161. I. CONJUNCTIONS JOIN SENTENCES together or OPPOSE them to each other.

John went to school, and Harry returned home.

And joins together the two sentences, *John went to school, Harry returned home.*

John went to school, but Harry returned home.

But opposes the two sentences to each other.

If the same verb applies to more than one sentence it is often only expressed once.

John and Harry went to school.

There are here in fact two sentences, *John went to school, Harry went to school,* which the Conjunction *and* joins together.

The man is honest and true is equivalent to *the man is honest and* the man is *true.*

§ 162. The Conjunction *and* sometimes seems to join words together.

Bread and milk is wholesome food.

Bread and milk is a compound, *and* joins *milk* to *bread.*

Give me the blue and white handkerchief.

Blue and white is the compound colour of the handkerchief.

This usage of Conjunctions may however be thought to arise from shortened forms of expressions.

Thus, *bread and milk* is *the food* which is (partly) *bread and* is (partly) *milk.*

The blue and white handkerchief is *the handkerchief* which is (partly) *blue and* is (partly) *white.*

There is a similar use of *or.*

Ambition or a desire of fame is such a principle, i. e. What is called *ambition or* is called *a desire of fame.*

§ 163. Some Conjunctions are used in pairs to make a kind of double junction or opposition.

Such are *both, and—either, or—neither, nor—as, as—whether, or.*

England flourished both under Elizabeth and under Anne.

The two sentences, *England flourished under Elizabeth, England flourished under Anne,* are joined doubly by *both* and by *and. Both* joins the former sentence to the latter. *And* joins the latter sentence to the former.

Either Mary or Elizabeth must have perished.

Either opposes *Mary must have perished* to *Elizabeth must have perished. Or* opposes *Elizabeth must have perished* to *Mary must have perished.*

He was as fierce as a lion.

He was fierce, a lion is fierce, these two are joined together in comparison by the two Conjunctions *as, as.*

Hence comes the common phrase *as well as.*

There are pleasures at school as well as at home, i. e. *there are as well pleasures at school as* there are pleasures *at home.*

The *as, as* are double Conjunctions.

The former Conjunction in each of these pairs cannot be used without the latter.

§ 164. Whenever there are words which belong alike to two branches of a sentence, care must be taken that each branch, together with the common part, forms a perfect sentence.

I speak and think of my friend: *of my friend* is common to the two branches.

I speak of my friend and *I think of my friend* are each of them a perfect sentence.

But we must not say *I allude and think of my friend*, because with *I allude* we require *to my friend*.

Therefore we say *I allude to and think of my friend*: *my friend* is the common part.

In the same way *he never can and never will speak of it* is correct. *He never has and never will speak of it* is incorrect. It should be *he never has spoken and never will speak*.

> *England flourished both under Elizabeth and under Anne.*

England flourished is common to both sentences.

We might have said *England flourished under both Elizabeth and Anne*; then *England flourished under* is the common part of the sentence. It is not correct to say *England flourished both under Elizabeth and Anne.*

Thus in the case of the relative pronoun it is correct to say *the thing which I heard and saw*, *which* being an objective belonging properly to both verbs; *which I heard and* which *I saw*, but it is incorrect to say *which I heard and was seen* for *which I heard and which was seen*, because the former *which* is an objective and the latter a nominative.

§ 165. The demonstrative pronoun *that* is often used as a Conjunction.

They told me that he was come.

The reason is that *that* marks out the sentence which follows it as the thing spoken of.

They told me that, viz. his-being-come.

The Conjunction *that* is often omitted but understood.

They told me he would obey, i. e. *they told me* that *he would obey*. See § 131.

§ 166. Some particles are used either as prepositions or Conjunctions. Such are *for*, *before*, *after*.

This may be explained by a reference to *for*.

For is a preposition marking the relation of *cause*; the cause being expressed by a substantive in the objective case, *I praise him for his valour*. But if a fact stated as a sentence is the *cause*, this sentence takes the place of the substantive, and *for* joins it to the principal sentence, and so acts as a Conjunction.

I praise him, for he is valorous. Here *for* is a Conjunction.

Sometimes in older writers *for that*, *before that*, *after that* are used.

He went away before that I spoke, i. e. *before that*, viz. my speaking.

There are other Conjunctions, *if*, *although*, *ere*, *until*, and the like.

All these join sentences together.

The sentences joined by such Conjunctions are dependent upon some principal sentence.

§ 167. Certain words in the sentences where Conjunctions occur are often omitted.

Such omissions are called ELLIPSES, and the sentences where they are found are called ELLIPTICAL.

He was as fierce as a lion, i. e. *as a lion is.*

As a lion is an *elliptical* sentence; there is an *ellipse* of the verb *is.*

The mistress praised Jane as well as him, i. e. *as well as* praised *him.*

Jowler liked Willy better than me, i. e. *than* he liked *me.*

Observe that the case which follows *than, as well as*, and such conjunctions, depends upon the way in which the sentence is to be filled up.

The mistress praised Jane as well as he would mean, *the mistress praised Jane as well as he* praised Jane.

Jowler liked Willy better than I would mean, *Jowler liked Willy better than I* liked Willy.

Than is not used with a relative pronoun, except by writers who imitate Latin construction. When it does occur, the pronoun is in the Objective; *than whom*, never *than who*.

Belial came last, than whom a spirit more lewd
Fell not from Heaven.—Milton.

Here *than* seems to be used as a preposition.

Nor hope to be myself less miserable
By what I seek, but others to make such
As I, i. e. *as I* am.—Milton.

The infinitive is often omitted after auxiliaries.

Have you seen him? I have, i. e. seen him.

Listen, if you will, i. e. *will* listen.

You will rejoice as I do[1], i. e. *do* rejoice.

[1] This usage of *do* may however be explained in another way. Since *do* expresses *action* generally, the verb may be employed to refer to any action. *You will rejoice as I act*: the *action* being of course that

But such omissions of the infinitive as *Sit where I told you to* for *to* sit are quite improper. We must either say *Sit where I told you* or *Sit where I told you to sit.*

There is a common form of ellipse, in which the participle follows the Conjunctions *if*, *although*, and the like.

I will come if summoned, i.e. *if* I am *summoned.*

He fell into mischief though often warned, i.e. *though* he was *often warned.*

§ 168. A Conjunction must in general stand at the beginning of the sentence which it joins, but the dependent sentence may either precede or stand in the midst of the principal sentence.

And the Sea-horse, though the ocean
Yield him no domestic cave,
Slumbers without sense of motion.

This sentence arranged in the most re-

of rejoicing. Thus we say, *You will rejoice as I have done*, where there is no ellipse, but *done* refers to the *action* of rejoicing.

gular form would stand thus: *And the Sea-horse slumbers without sense of motion, though the ocean yield him no domestic cave.*

On Conjunctive Adverbs, see § 175.

CHAPTER XVI.

SYNTAX OF ADVERBS.

§ 169. I. ADVERBS of TIME, MANNER, OR PLACE qualify VERBS OR PARTICIPLES.

He then declared. Having spoken thus. We stopped here.

It should be remembered that the Adverbs *here, there, where,* mark *at* a place; *hither, thither, whither,* mark *to* a place; *hence, thence, whence,* mark *from* a place.

Where do you live? I came hither. I am going thence.

It is not uncommon to say, *Where are you going?* for, *Whither are you going?*

I came here for *I came hither*, and the like; but such usage is incorrect.

In such phrases as *formerly beautiful*, *now important*, the Adverbs seem to qualify adjectives, but really there is an ellipse, as having *formerly* been *beautiful*, being *now important*.

§ 170. II. ADVERBS of DEGREE qualify ADJECTIVES or other ADVERBS.

Very great, *too slightly*, *extremely great.*

We cannot say, *I very love*; we may say, *I love extremely*, because *extremely* may be used either as an Adverb of manner or as an Adverb of degree.

The Adverbs, *so*, *thus*, *scarcely*, and many others, may be used either as of degree or of manner.

§ 171. The negative Adverb *not* may qualify either verbs, adjectives, or adverbs.

Two negatives make an affirmative.

I cannot not observe, i. e. I must observe.

An Adverb is said to be *adverbial* to the word which it qualifies.

I know this very well.

Very is adverbial to *well,* and *well* is adverbial to *know.*

§ 172. III. PREPOSITIONS, when not followed by a substantive, are used as ADVERBS.

I went on. They came up. She walked in.

They are not worth speaking to. The participle *speaking* and the preposition *to* used adverbially forms a compound which means *addressing.* The participle is used like a substantive after *worth.*

A box to sleep in. The infinitive *sleep* and the preposition *in* used adverbially form a compound—*sleep in;* which is an infinitive used as a substantive, and joined to *box* by the preposition *to.*

§ 173. We now see that some particles are used either as prepositions, conjunctions, or Adverbs. See § 166.

1. As prepositions, when followed by a substantive.

He went away after my coming.

2. As conjunctions, when followed by a sentence.

He went away after I came.

3. As Adverbs, when not followed either by a substantive or by a sentence.

He went away. I came after.

§ 174. The use of the particle *but* deserves special notice.

In old English there were two distinct particles.

1. *But* (connected with *to boot*). Hence comes the conjunction *but* in common use.

I came, but he went.

2. *But* (*be-out*) signifying *without, except*, used either as a preposition, conjunction, or Adverb.

Hence comes the *but* which is still used in the following ways:—

1. As a preposition.

Thou shalt have none other gods but Me, i. e. except *Me*.

I cannot but speak, i. e. *I cannot* remain without *speaking.*

Speak is infinitive governed by the preposition *but.*

2. As a conjunction.

There should be no king but he, i. e. *there should be no king* except he were king.

Away went Gilpin—who but he? i. e. *who* went, *unless* he went?

God is light,
And never but in unapproached light
Dwelt from eternity.—Milton.

But is here a conjunction equivalent to *except.*

3. As an Adverb.

There would be but small improvements, i. e. only *small improvements.*

I can but speak, i. e. only *speak.*

This usage of *but* may be traced to its use as a conjunction. Ancient writers have *There is not but one*, i. e. *there is not* any except there is *one.* Modern writers say, *There is but one*, omitting the negative.

Hence *but* is equivalent to *only*. According to modern usage, *I cannot but speak* means I cannot *forbear speaking; I can but speak* means *I can* only *speak*.

§ 175. IV. CONJUNCTIVE ADVERBS perform the part both of ADVERBS and of CONJUNCTIONS.

Such are *neither*, *nor*, and the relative adverbs *when*, *where*, &c.

Neither I nor John will come, i. e. both *I will not come* and *John* will not come.

Neither and *nor* are adverbial to the verb *come*, and oppose the two sentences one to the other.

I was speaking when John came.

When marks the time of *came*, and so is adverbial to it, and also joins *John came* to *I was speaking*.

§ 176. There are certain Adverbs which are commonly placed at the beginning of sentences, and form a kind of connecting link between two sentences.

Such are *however, nevertheless, notwithstanding, accordingly*. *So, now*, and *then*, are often used in this way without marking very decidedly either manner or time.

Now there was much grass in the place. So the men sat down in number about five thousand.

§ 177. Some Adverbs are used to lay some stress upon particular words in a sentence. Such are *even, also, too*. *Even* precedes the word to which it refers; *also* and *too* follow it.

Even John spoke. John also spoke. John too spoke.

In each instance *John* is the word qualified.

§ 178. An Adverb may either precede or follow the word which it qualifies. According to the regular order they follow verbs, and procede adjectives.

I love you extremely. This is extremely beautiful. You do this rather skilfully.

The position of an Adverb qualifying a verb is very frequently changed.

Observe that in the last sentence *frequently* is adverbial to *changed*, but stands before it.

§ 179. INTERJECTIONS are inserted without being connected, by way of construction, with the other words of a sentence. In such sentences as *O, that this were so!* *that* does not join its sentence to *O*, but to *I wish* understood.

CHAPTER XVII.

SUMMARY OF THE RULES OF SYNTAX.

1. *Syntax of the Nominative.*

§ 180. I. THE Nominative is the subject of some verb.

II. The Nominative is used after the verb *to be* or its participles.

III. The Nominative is used in apposition.

IV. The Nominative is used with a participle, no verb being understood.

V. The Nominative is used when a person is spoken to.

2. *Syntax of the Possessive.*

I. The Possessive is governed by a substantive, and marks the person or thing to which that substantive belongs.

II. The Possessive is used in apposition.

3. *Syntax of the Objective.*

I. The Objective is governed by some transitive verb, and marks the object of that verb.

II. The Objective is used after some intransitive verbs when its meaning is akin to that of the verb.

III. The Objective is governed by the adjective *like* and by prepositions.

IV. The Objective is used in apposition.

V. The Objective is used to measure time or space.

4. *Syntax of Adjectives.*

I. An Adjective is used with some substantive which it qualifies.

II. An Adjective stands alone after the verbs *am*, *become*, and the like, and their participles.

III. An Adjective with the definite article has sometimes its substantive omitted but understood.

IV. An Adjective with the definite article is used to express an abstract quality.

V. Some few Adjectives are used like adverbs.

5. *Syntax of Pronouns.*

I. Adjectival Pronouns are used with a substantive expressed.

II. Adjectival Pronouns stand alone, but some substantive is understood.

6. *Syntax of Relative and Interrogative Pronouns.*

I. A Relative Pronoun agrees with its

Antecedent in gender and number, but not in case.

II. The case of a Relative Pronoun depends upon the sentence to which it belongs.

III. Interrogative Pronouns have no Antecedent, but they are used in their own sentences like the relatives, which are the same in form.

7. *Syntax of the Articles.*

I. The Indefinite Article marks that there is a class of which some one is taken.

II. The Definite Article is used to distinguish its noun from some others of its class.

8. *Syntax of the Verb.*

I. A finite Verb, when used transitively, has an object expressed or understood.

II. A Verb agrees with its subject in number and in person.

9. *Syntax of the Subjunctive Mood.*

I. The Subjunctive Mood, in dependent sentences, is used to express an uncertain event.

II. The Subjunctive is used to express a conditional event.

III. The Subjunctive is used to supply the place of the third person of the imperative mood.

10. *Syntax of the Infinitive Mood.*

I. A verb in the Infinitive Mood is used as a substantive.

II. When one verb follows another it is in the Infinitive.

III. The Infinitive may have its object and its adjuncts.

11. *Syntax of the Participles.*

I. Participles, whether present or past, are used as adjectives.

II. The Present Participle of a transitive verb may be followed by an object.

III. The Present Participle is often used as a substantive.

IV. Some Present Participles are used like prepositions.

V. The Past Participle when used with the auxiliary *have* has an active sense.

12. *Syntax of Prepositions.*

I. A Preposition is followed by a substantive or some word used as a substantive.

II. A Preposition marks the relation of the word which it governs to some other word in the sentence.

13. *Syntax of Conjunctions.*

Conjunctions join sentences together or oppose them to each other.

14. *Syntax of Adverbs.*

I. Adverbs of time, manner, or place, qualify verbs or participles.

II. Adverbs of degree qualify adjectives or other adverbs.

III. Prepositions, when not followed by a substantive, are used as Adverbs.

IV. Conjunctive Adverbs perform the part of adverbs and of conjunctions.

CHAPTER XVIII.

PARSING.

§ 181. To PARSE is to give an account of each word in a sentence, both as to its form and as to its construction.

The following examples will explain how this is to be done.

The abbreviations employed will be easily understood.

Observe, that since the verb expresses the action in a sentence, we say for convenience-sake that a conjunction joins the *verb*, meaning the *sentence* to which the verb belongs.

1. We thought, as we hollow'd his narrow bed
And smoothed down his lonely pillow,
The foe and the stranger would tread o'er his head,
And we far away on the billow.

Wolfe.

we . . . . pronoun of 1st person, plural nominative, subject of *thought.*

thought. . verb active, indicative past, 1st pers. plur., from *think*, agreeing with its subject *we.*

as . . . . conjunction, joining *hollowed* to *thought.*

we . . . . subject of *hollowed.*

hollowed . verb act., indic. past, 1st pers. plur., from *hollow*, agreeing with its subject *we.*

his . . . . pronoun of 3rd person, sing. possessive, dependent on *bed.*

narrow . . adjective, qualifying *bed.*

bed . . . . substantive, sing. objective, object of *hollowed.*

and . . . conjunction, joining *smoothed* to *hollowed.*

smoothed . verb act., indic. past, 1st pers. plur., from *smooth*, agreeing with its subject *we* understood.

down . . . adverb, adverbial to *smoothed.*

his . . . . dependent on *pillow.*

lonely . . adjective, qualifying *pillow.*

pillow . . substantive, sing. object., object of *smoothed.*

The conjunction *that* is understood before *the foe*, i. e. *we thought* that *the foe.* This conjunction would join *would tread* to *thought.*

the . . . . definite article, defining *foe.*

foe . . . . substantive, sing. nom., subject of *would.*

and . . . conjunction, joining *stranger* to *foe*.

the . . . . defining *stranger*.

stranger . substantive, sing. nom., subject of *would*.

would . . verb act., indic. past, 3rd pers. plur., from *will*, agreeing with the subject *they* understood from *foe* and *stranger*.

tread . . . verb act., infin. pres., following *would*.

o'er. . . . preposition, governing *head*, joining it to *tread*.

his . . . . dependent on *head*.

head . . substantive, sing. object., governed by *o'er*.

and . . . joining *should be* understood to *would tread*.

we . . . . subject of *should be* understood.

far . . . adverbial to *away*.

away . . . adverb, adverbial to *should be* understood; *we* should be *far away* is the full sentence.

on . . . . preposition, governing *billow*, joining it to *should be* understood.

the . . . . defining *billow*.

billow . . substantive, sing. object., governed by *on*.

2. Quoth Mistress Gilpin, That's well said,
And, for that wine is dear,
We will be furnished with our own,
Which is both bright and clear.

Cowper.

quoth . . verb act., indic. pres., 3rd pers. sing. (from an old verb not now in use), agreeing with its subject *Mistress Gilpin*.

Mistress Gilpin } singular nominatives in apposition, subject of the verb *quoth*.

that's . . . for *that is*.

that . . . demonstrative pron., sing. nom., subject of *is*.

is . . . . verb, indic. pres., 3rd pers. sing., from *be*, agreeing with *that*.

well . . . adverb, adverbial to *said*.

said . . . past participle, from the verb *say*, following *is*.

Observe, that *is said* together make up the passive indicative present of the verb *say*.

and . . . conjunction, joining *will be furnished* to *is said*.

for that . used instead of *for*, conjunction, joining *is* to *will be furnished*.

wine . . . substantive, nom. sing., subject of *is*.

is . . . . agreeing with *wine*.

dear . . . adjective, qualifying *wine*.

we . . . . pronoun of 1st person plur. nom., subject of *will*.

will . . . verb act., ind. pres., 1st pers. plur., agreeing with *we*.

be . . . . verb, infin. pres., from *be*, following the verb *will*.

furnished. past part., from *furnish*, following *be*.

Observe, that *will be furnished* together

make up the passive indicative future of the verb *furnish.*

with . . . preposition, governing *wine* understood, joining *our own* to *furnished.*

our . . . possessive from *we,* dependent on *wine* understood.

own . . . adjectival pronoun, referring to *wine* understood, object., governed by *with.*

which . . relative pronoun, referring to antecedent *wine;* joining *is* to *will be furnished;* sing. nom., subject of *is.*

is . . . . agreeing with *which.*

both . . . conjunction, joining *bright* to *clear.*

bright . . adjective, qualifying *which.*

and . . . joining *clear* to *bright.*

clear . . . adjective, qualifying *which.*

3. So is the sinner's hope cut off,
Or, if it transient rise,

'Tis like the spider's airy web
From every breath that flies.
Logan.

so . . . . adverb, adverbial to *cut*.

is . . . . verb, indic. pres., 3rd pers. sing., agreeing with its subject *hope*.

the . . . . def. article, defining *sinner's*.

sinner's . substantive, possess. sing., dependent on *hope*.

hope . . . substantive, nom. sing., subject of *is*.

cut . . . . past participle, from the verb *cut*, following *is*.

Is cut together make up pass. indic. pres., 3rd pers. sing., of *cut*.

off . . . . adverb, adverbial to *cut*.

or . . . . conjunction, joining *it is like* to *is cut off*.

if . . . . conjunction, joining *rise* to *it is like*.

it . . . . pronoun of 3rd person, nom. sing., subject of *rise*.

transient . adjective, qualifying *it*.

rise . . . verb act., subjunct. pres., 3rd pers. sing., from *rise*, agreeing with *it*.

'tis . . . . for *it is*.

it . . . . subject of *is*.

is . . . . agreeing with *it*.

like . . . adjective, qualifying *it*.

the . . . . def. article, defining *spider's*.

spider's . substantive, possess. sing., dependent on *web*.

airy . . . adjective, qualifying *web*.

web . . . substantive, object. sing., governed by *like*.

from . . . preposition, governing *breath*, and joining it to *flies*.

every . . indefinite pronoun, qualifying *breath*.

breath . . substantive, object. sing., governed by *from*.

that . . . relative pronoun, referring to

the antecedent *web*; joining *flies* to *is*; nomin. sing., subject of *flies*.

flies . . . verb act., indic. pres., 3rd pers. sing., from *fly*, agreeing with *that*.

ELLIPSES.

§ 182. The meaning of the words ELLIPSE and ELLIPTICAL has been explained in § 167.

In order to understand a sentence perfectly, we should be able to supply every Ellipse in it. The most common sentences are often Elliptical. It will therefore be useful to examine a sentence, in order to show where it is Elliptical, and how the Ellipses are to be supplied.

(*a*) "It was necessary for the world, that arts should be invented and improved, books written and transmitted to posterity, nations conquered and civilized: now since the proper and genuine motives to these and the like great actions, would only influence virtuous minds; (*b*) there would be but small improvements in the world, were there not some common principle of action working equally with all men. (*c*) And such a principle is ambition or a desire of fame, by which great endowments are not suffered to lie idle and useless to the public, and many vicious men overreached, as it were, and engaged contrary to their natural inclinations in a glorious and laudable course of action. For we may farther observe, that men of the greatest abilities are most fired with ambition. (*d*) And that, on the contrary, mean and narrow minds are the least actuated by it; whether it be that a man's sense of his own incapacities makes him despair of coming at fame, or that he has not enough range of thought to look out for any good which does not more immediately relate to his interest or convenience, or that Providence in the very frame of his soul, would not subject him to such a passion as would be useless to the world, and a torment to himself."—ADDISON.

The sentences are marked (*a*), (*b*), &c., that they may be examined separately. The words to be supplied are printed in Italics.

(*a*) It was necessary for the world that arts should be invented, and *it was necessary for the world that arts should be* improved, *it was necessary for the world that* books *should be* written, and *it was necessary for the world that books should be* transmitted to posterity, *it was necessary for the world that* nations *should be* conquered, and *it was necessary for the world that* nations *should be* civilized.

Hence we see that the first "and" joins *it was necessary* (understood) to "it was necessary;" "books" is nominative, subject of *should be* (understood), and "nations" is nominative, subject of *should be* (understood). Thus we must supply Ellipses, in order to parse correctly.

(*b*) There would be *nothing* but small improvements in the world, *if* there were not some common principle of action working equally with all men.

On the usage of *but* see § 174. "Were there not," the order is altered, because *if* is understood. § 124.

(*c*) And such a principle is *what is called* ambition, or *is called* desire of fame, by which *principle* great endowments are not suffered to lie idle and useless to the public, and *ambition or desire of fame is a principle by which* many vicious men *are* overreached, *so* as it were *to be overreached*, and *ambition or desire of fame is a principle by which many vicious men are* engaged contrary to their inclinations in many great and glorious actions.

On the use of *or* and of the last *and* see § 162. "As it were." "Were" is here put for *would be* or *might be.* See § 125. The pronoun "it" refers to the case of *being overreached:* "as" indicates an Ellipse of *so*, and joins "it were" to the sentence to which *so* belongs. "As it were" is equivalent to *in such a manner as it might be to be overreached.* It is thus that the Elliptical phrase *as it were* has come to be equivalent to *after a sort of manner.*

(*d*) And *we may further observe* that, on the contrary, mean and narrow minds are least actuated by it, whether it (*the reason why mean minds are least actuated by ambition*) be that a man's sense of his own incapacities makes him despair of coming to fame, or *it be* that he has not enough range of thought to look out for any good, which does not more immediately relate to his interest, or *to look out for any good which does not more immediately relate to his* convenience, or *it be* that Providence, in the very frame of his soul, would not subject him to such a passion as *that passion is which* would be useless to the world, and *would be* a torment to himself.

APPENDIX I.

PREFIXES AND AFFIXES.

§ 183. WORDS are altered to suit them to the various purposes of speech by adding to them syllables or other words.

The *body* of the word, i.e. the part which contains the main sense, is called the Root or Radical part. This main sense is altered by the additions which are made to the body of the word.

Words or syllables placed before the main body of the word are called Prefixes.

The Prefixes are subject to variations in form according to the consonant which follows them; *ad*verse, *ac*cept, *ag*grieve, *al*lay, *ar*rive, *as*sent, *at*tract, have all the same Prefix.

Additions at the end of the word are called Affixes.

E. g. 1. *sharp* is an adjective.
sharp-en is a verb.
sharp-er is a substantive, and also the comparative degree of "sharp."
sharp-ly is an adverb.

The syllables *en*, *er*, *ly*, are Affixes which alter the meaning of "sharp."

2. "*pose*" is a verb derived from Latin, which means "place," from which we have, *ap*-pose, place *near*; *op*-pose, place *against*; *com*-pose, place *together*; *inter*-pose, place *between*; *de*-pose, place *down*; *dis*-pose, place *in order*; *sup*-pose, place *under*, &c. The words *ap-*, *op-*, *com-*, *inter-*, &c., are Latin prepositions, and when thus set before words are called Prefixes.

§ 184. The following are some of the Prefixes and Affixes which are most commonly in use. They belong chiefly to three languages, English, Latin, Greek. Many of them are prepositions.

A. ENGLISH PREFIXES.

A, signifying		*on*,	as	*a*shore.
Be	,,	*about*,	,,	*be*fal.
En (*em*)	,,	*to make*,	,,	*em*power.
For	,,	*denial*,	,,	*for*bid, *for*give.
Fore	,,	*before*,	,,	*fore*tel.
Gain	,,	*contrary*,	,,	*gain*say.
Mis	,,	*error*,	,,	*mis*take.
Out	,,	*beyond*,	,,	*out*run.
Over	,,	*above*,	,,	*over*flow.
Un	,,	*not*,	,,	*un*do.
Under	,,	*below*,	,,	*under*value.
Up	,,		,,	*up*set.
With	,,	*against*,	,,	*with*stand.

B. LATIN PREFIXES.

These are chiefly prepositions, and the words to which they are prefixed are also themselves mostly derived from the Latin.

A	*from*	*a*verse.
Ad (*ac*, *af*, *ag*, *al*, *an*, *ap*, *ar*, *as*, *at*)	*to*	*ad*join, *af*fect, *an*nex, *ap*prove.
Am (*amb*)	*around*	*amb*ient.

Ante	*before*	*anti*cipate.
Circum (*circu*)	*round*	*circum*ference.
Con (*co*, *col*, *com*, *cor*)	*together*	*con*gregate, *co*eval, *col*lect, *com*pare, *cor*rupt.
Contra	*against*	*contra*dict.
De	*down*	*de*cide.
Dis or *Di* (*dif*)	*asunder*	*dis*appoint, *dif*fer.
Ex or *E* (*ef*)	*out*	*ex*pel, *ef*fect.
Extra	*beyond*	*extra*ordinary.
In (*i*, *il*, *im*, *ir*)	*into* (before a verb)	*in*fuse, *i*gnore, *il*lude, *im*prove, *ir*ritate.
———	*not* (before an adjective)	*in*finite, *i*gnorant, *il*legal, *im*mense, *ir*rational.
Inter	*between*	*inter*cept.
Intra	*within*	*intra*mural.
Intro	*inwards*	*intro*duce.
Ob (*oc*, *of*, *op*)	*at*	*ob*ject, *oc*cur, *of*fend, *op*pose.
Per (*pel*)	*through*	*per*vert, *pel*lucid.
Post	*after*	*post*pone.
Pre	*before*	*pre*dict.
Pro (*pur*)	*forward*	*pro*mote, *pur*pose.
Re or *Retro*	*back*	*re*cede, *retro*grade.

Se	*apart*	*se*lect.
Sine	*without*	*sine*cure.
Sub or *Subter* (*suc*, *suf*, *sug*, *sup*, *sus*)	*under*	*sub*tract, *suc*cour, *suf*fer, *sug*gest, *sup*port, *sus*pend, *subter*fuge.
Super (*sur*)	*over*	*super*fluous, *sur*vive.
Trans (*tra*)	*across*	*trans*port, *tra*duce.
Ultra	*beyond*	*ultra*marine.

C. GREEK PREFIXES.

A or *An*	*without*	*a*pathy, *an*archy.
Amphi	*on both sides*	*amphi*theatre.
Ana	*back*	*ana*lyse.
Anti (*ant*)	*against*	*anti*pathy, *ant*arctic.
Apo (*aph*)	*away*	*apo*state, *aph*elion.
Cata (*cat*, *cath*)	*down, utterly*	*cata*strophe, *cat*echize, *cath*olic.
Dia	*through*	*dia*meter.
En	*on*	*en*ergy.
Epi (*ep*, *eph*)	*on*	*epi*taph, *ep*och, *eph*emeral.
Ex	*out*	*ex*odus.
Hyper	*over*	*hyper*bole.
Hypo	*under*	*hypo*crite.

Meta (*meth*)	*change*	*meta*morphose, *meth*od.
Para	*beside*	*para*ble.
Peri	*round*	*peri*od.
Syn, *sy*, *syl*, *sym*)	*with*	*syn*tax, *sy*stem, *syl*lable, *sym*pathy.

II. AFFIXES.

A. To Substantives, marking the agent or doer.

-an	histori*an*	*-ent*	stud*ent*
-ant	serv*ant*	*-er*	garden*er*
-ar	li*ar*	*-ess*	govern*ess*
-ard	stew*ard*	*-ist*	agricultur*ist*
-ary	mission*ary*	*-ster*	barri*ster*
-eer	auction*eer*	*-tor*	vic*tor*.

State or quality.

-acy	prim*acy*.	*-mony*	patri*mony*
-age	bond*age*	*-ness*	like*ness*
-ce	ignoran*ce*	*-ric*	bishop*ric*
-dom	king*dom*	*-ship*	wor*ship*
-head or *-hood*	God*head*, man*hood*	*-tude*	soli*tude*
-ism	sch*ism*	*-ure*	ten*ure*
-ment	monu*ment*	*-ty*	quanti*ty*
		-y	agenc*y*.

Act of doing, or thing done.

-tion or *sion* — ac*tion*, declen*sion*.

Little or young.

-cle	ici*cle*	*-let*	brace*let*
-cule	animal*cule*	*-ling*	duck*ling*
-et	flowr*et*	*-ock*	hill*ock*.
-kin	lamb*kin*		

Place of.

-ary, *-ery*, or *-ory* — gran*ary*, rook*ery*, deposit*ory*.

deposit*ory*	means	the place where	a thing is deposited.
deposit*ary*	means	the person with whom	

B. Adjectives marking of or belonging to.

-al	roy*al*	*-ic*	com*ic*
-an	hum*an*	*-ical*	com*ical*
-ane	hum*ane*	*-id*	splend*id*
-ar	lun*ar*	*-ine*	mar*ine*
-ary	prim*ary*	*-ish*	fool*ish*.

Consisting of.		Made of.	
-aceous	farin*aceous*	*-en*	wood*en*.

Full of.

-eous	bount*eous*	*-ous*	por*ous*
-ful	fruit*ful*	*-some*	frolic*some*
-ose	verb*ose*	*-y*	hill*y*.

Being.

-ant	luxuri*ant*	*-ent*	depend*ent*.

Being in a state of.

-ate	passion*ate*	*-ete*	compl*ete*
-ed	wretch*ed*	*-ite*	pol*ite*.

Able to do.

-acious	cap*acious*	*-ive*	destruct*ive*.

Able to be done.

-able	toler*able*	*-ible*	destruct*ible*
-ble	no*ble*	*-ile*	duct*ile*.

Little.

-ish whit*ish*

Wanting.

-less care*less*.

Repeated.

-fold mani*fold*

Towards.

-ward for*ward*.

Like.

-like	war*like*	*-ly*	good*ly*.

C. Verbs.

-ate	anim*ate*	*-ish*	publ*ish*
-en	sharp*en*	*-ise* or *-ize*	exerc*ise*,
-fy	puri*fy*		bapt*ize*.

D. Adverbs.

-ly	soft*ly*	*-ward* or	back*ward*,
-ce	on*ce*	*-wards*	to*wards*
-times	often*times*	*-wise*	like*wise*.

APPENDIX II.

GRAMMATICAL TERMS, WITH THEIR DERIVATIONS.

§ 184. The following words are derived from the Latin, unless it is otherwise expressed.

; means *derived from*.

Absolute; *ab*, from, *solvere*, to loose.

Abstract; *abs*, from, *trahere*, to draw.

Accent, *accentus; ad*, to, *canere*, to sing.

Accidence, *accidentia; accidere*, to happen. Accidence concerns the changes of form which *happen* to words.

Active (voice), (*vox*) *activa; agere*, to do.

Adverb, *adverbium; ad*, to, *verbum*, verb. Adverbs are commonly added to verbs.

Adjunct, *adjunctum; ad*, to, *jungere*, to join.

Alphabet; *alpha, beta*, Greek names for A, B.

Apostrophe; (Greek) *apo*, from, *strephein*, to turn.

Apposition, *appositio; ad*, to, *ponere*, to place.

Article, *articulus*, small joint.

Aspirate, *aspiratus; ad*, to, *spirare*, to breathe.

Attribute, *attributum; ad*, to, *tribuere*, to give.

Auxiliary (verb), (*verbum*) *auxiliare; auxilium*, help.

Capital, *capitalis; caput*, head.

Cardinal (number), (*numerus*) *cardinalis; cardo*, a hinge. Cardinal are chief numbers.

Case, *casus; cadere*, to fall. The different cases *fall*, as it were, or are derived from one stem.

Clause, *clausula; claudere*, to close.

Collective; *con*, together, *legere*, to gather.

Common, *communis*.

Comparative (degree), (*gradus*) *comparativus; comparare*, to compare.

Concord, *concordia; concors*, agreeing.

Conjugate, *conjugare; con*, together, *jugum*, yoke.

Conjunction, *conjunctio; con*, together, *jungere*, to join.

Consonant, *consonans; con*, together, *sonare*, to sound.

Copula, *copula*, a tie.

Declension, *declensio; declinare*, to slope down. The different cases *decline*, as it were, from the nominative.

Defective (verb), (*verbum*) *defectivum; deficere*, to be deficient.

Definite (article), (*articulus*) *definitus; de*, down, *finire*, to limit.

Demonstrative (pronoun), (*pronomen*) *demonstrativum; de*, down, *monstrare*, to show.

Diphthong, *diphthongus*; (Greek) *dis*, twice, *phthongus*, sound.

Dissyllable; (Greek) *dis*, twice, *syllabe*, syllable.

Ellipse, *ellipsis*; (Greek) *elleipein*, to be wanting.

Emphasis, *emphasis*; (Greek) *en*, upon, *phanai*, to say.

Feminine (gender), (*genus*) *fœmininum*; *fœmina*, woman.

Future (tense), (*tempus*) *futurum*; *futurus*, about to be.

Gender, *genus*, kind.

Grammar, *grammatice*; (Greek) *grammata*, letters. Grammar is concerned with *letters*, and words composed of them.

Hyphen; *hypo*, under, *hen*, one (Greek).

Imperative (mood), (*modus*) *imperativus*; *imperare*, to command.

Impersonal (verb), (*verbum*) *impersonale*; *in*, not, *persona*, person.

Indicative (mood), (*modus*) *indicativus*; *indicare*, to point out.

Infinitive (mood), (*modus*) *infinitivus*; *in*, not, *finitus*, finite.

Interrogative (pronoun), (*pronomen*) *interrogativum*; *interrogare*, to question.

Interjection, *interjectio*; *inter*, between, *jacere*, to throw.

Italic (letter), (*litera*) *Italica*; *Italia*, Italy.

Language, *lingua*, tongue.

Masculine (gender), (*genus*) *masculinum; masculus*, male.

Monosyllable; *monos*, alone, *syllabe*, syllable (Greek).

Mood, *modus*, manner.

Neuter (Gender), (*genus*) *neutrum*, neither of the two.

Nominative (case), (*casus*) *nominativus; nominare*, to name.

Noun, *nomen*, name.

Noun adjective, *nomen adjectivum; ad*, to, *jacere*, to throw.

Noun substantive, *nomen substantivum; substantia*, substance.

Number, *numerus*.

Numeral, *numeralis; numerus*, number.

Object, *objectum; ob*, at, *jacere*, to throw.

Objective (case), (*casus*) *objectivus; objectum*, object.

Ordinal (number), (*numerus*) *ordinalis; ordo*, order. An ordinal number marks the *order* of a person or thing.

Parenthesis; *para*, beside, *en*, in, *thesis*, placing (Greek).

Participle, *participium; pars*, part, *capere*, to take.

Particle, *particula*, small part.

Partitive, *pars*, part.

Passive (voice), (*vox*) *passiva* ; *pati*, to suffer.

Past (tense), (Engl.) pass.

Perfect (tense), (*tempus*) *perfectum* ; *per*, through, *facere*, to make.

Personal (pronoun), (*pronomen*) *personale* ; *persona*, person.

Phrase ; (Greek) *phrazein*, to speak.

Pluperfect (tense), (*tempus*) *plusquam perfectum* ; *plus*, more, *quam*, than, *perfectus*, perfect.

Plural (number), (*numerus*) *pluralis* ; *plures*, many.

Polysyllable ; (Greek) *polys*, many, *syllabe*, syllable.

Positive (degree), (*gradus*) *positivus* ; *ponere*, to place.

Possessive (case), (*casus*) *possessivus* ; *possidere*, to possess.

Potential (mood), (*modus*) *potentialis* ; *potens*, able.

Predicate, *prædicatum* ; *prædicare*, to assert.

Preposition, *præpositio* ; *præ*, before, *ponere*, to place.

Pronoun, *pronomen* ; *pro*, instead of, *nomen*, name.

Relative (pronoun), (*pronomen*) *relativum* ; *re*, back, *ferre*, to carry.

Roman (letter) (*litera*), *Romana* ; *Roma*, Rome.

Semivowel, *semivocalis* ; *semi*, half, *vox*, voice.

Singular (number), (*numerus*) *singularis*; *singuli*, one by one.

Subject, *subjectum* ; *sub*, under, *jacere*, to throw.

Subjunctive (mood), (*modus*) *subjunctivus* ; *sub*, under, *jungere*, to join.

Superlative (degree), (*gradus*) *superlativus*; *super*, above, *ferre*, to carry.

Syllable, *syllabe* ; (Greek) *syn*, together, *lambanein*, to take.

Syntax, *syntaxis* ; (Greek) *syn*, together, *tassein*, to arrange.

Tense, *tempus*, time.

Transitive (verb), *verbum transitivum* ; *transire*, to pass over.

Triphthong, *triphthongus* ; (Greek) *tris*, thrice, *phthongus*, sound.

Verb, *verbum*, word.

Voice, *vox*.

Vowel, *vocalis* ; *vox*, voice.

THE END.

GILBERT AND RIVINGTON, PRINTERS, ST. JOHN'S SQUARE, LONDON.